CONFESSIONS
of a
D.C. Madam

The Politics of Sex, Lies, and Blackmail

HENRY W. VINSON
with **Nick Bryant**

Published by:
Trine Day LLC
PO Box 577
Walterville, OR 97489
1-800-556-2012
www.TrineDay.com
publisher@TrineDay.net

Library of Congress Control Number: 2013937958

Vinson, Henry Walter
Cofessions of a D.C. Madam–1st ed.
p. cm.
Includes index and references.
Epub (ISBN-13) 978-1-937584-30-6
Mobi (ISBN-13) 978-1-937584-98-6
Print (ISBN-13) 978-1-937584-29-0
1. Vinson, Henry Walter. 2. Vinson, Henry Walter -- Trials, litigation, etc. 3. Escort services -- Washington (D.C. 4. Political corruption -- Washington (D.C.) -- Case studies. 5. Sex scandals -- Washington (D.C.) 6. Spence, Craig J. 7. King, Larry -- (Lawrence E.) I. Vinson, Henry Walter II. Title

First Edition
10 9 8 7 6 5 4 3 2 1

Printed in the USA
Distribution to the Trade by:
Independent Publishers Group (IPG)
814 North Franklin Street
Chicago, Illinois 60610
312.337.0747
www.ipgbook.com

Only the small secrets need to be protected. The large ones are kept secret by public incredulity.

– MARSHALL McLUHAN

TABLE OF CONTENTS

FOREWORD

*C*onfessions of a D.C. Madam lifts the veil on a facet of Americans politics that has been embargoed by the media: The sexual blackmailing of our power elite. If prostitution is indeed the world's oldest profession, politics is probably the world's second oldest profession. Or perhaps politics preceded prostitution, because it's conceivable that prehistoric hierarchies were established before sexual barter. Regardless of which profession emerged first, sexual blackmail seems to naturally tiptoe into their merger.

At first glance, Henry Vinson seems to be an unlikely harbinger of these secrets. Aristotle wrote, "Youth is easily deceived because it is quick to hope," and *Confessions of a D.C. Madam* chronicles the treacherous odyssey of Henry, whose youthful hope, ambition, and naiveté delivered him to the wrong place at the wrong time. Youthful sojourns to the wrong place at the wrong time aren't uncommon, but they're generally accompanied by a round trip ticket. So most ill-fated, youthful diversions are eventually righted and the vast majority of such sojourns have a tendency to culminate in adulthoods that unfold with the trappings of normalcy. Conversely, Henry's sojourn to the wrong place at the wrong would have enduring and dire consequences.

Henry came of age in rural West Virginia in the 1960s, and he was a shy, reserved kid, who had to quash the slightest traces of his sexuality. But as a 26-year-old, he became enmeshed in an extremely unlikely chain of events that ultimately transformed him from an unassuming, introverted mortician to the proprietor of a gay escort service in Washington, D.C. His unplanned and unforeseen metamorphosis was the product of the impetuousness of youth, and it occurred quite literally overnight.

Henry's youthful ambition and innate ingenuity enabled him to considerably enlarge his escort service. His ambition, however, was accompanied by an inexperience that didn't permit him to see that he was freefalling into an abyss that was forged by the most shadowy and sinister aspects of Washington, D.C., power politics. Henry eventually found himself ensconced by a cast of ominous characters, and he proved to be the perfect foil for their devious scheming, because he quickly found himself over his head.

Henry eventually encountered a sociopathic powerbroker who spent $20,000 a month on gay escorts for himself and his cronies. Although $20,000 a month augmented Henry's coffers, he came to the realization—albeit too late—that he had unwittingly entered into a Faustian pact. The powerbroker had connections to the elite strata of Washington, and a seeming hotline to Mount Olympus. He arranged midnight tours of the White House with male prostitutes in tow, and he had a cadre of operatives at his disposal. He also had a lavish house in an upscale D.C. neighborhood that was wired for audio and visual blackmail. Henry was a firsthand witness to the concealed cameras that were used to compromise the rich and powerful.

To Henry's shock and dismay, he would ultimately discover that elements of the American ruling class eclipse even Caligula's depravity. Young men and women and even children are merely sexual playthings for some of our country's power elite. When Henry became fully aware of the malevolent forces that had ensnared him, he attempted to escape their stranglehold, but he quickly realized that his Faustian pact didn't have an exit clause. His life was threatened, his family was terrorized, and he became a dispensable pawn in the ruthless game of power politics.

Although *Confessions of a D.C. Madam* gives the reader a rarefied glimpse into D.C. Babylon, the import of the book is its elucidation of the age-old story of sexual blackmail. Blackmailed powerbrokers and their blackmailers would never divulge the secrets that submerged Henry, so his story is unique in that he is definitely the man who knows too much, and he's alive to tell his tale. Although Henry's life has been spared, he's had to contend with the brazen malice of elements within the federal government who are resolved to never break the seal on the secrets Henry chanced upon.

Indeed, *Confessions of a D.C. Madam* shows the extraordinary measures that entities within the federal government are willing to take to ensure that such secrets remain a riddle wrapped in a mystery inside an enigma. Henry was twenty-nine years old when the government decided that the time was ripe to dismantle his escort service, and he was pounded with a 43-count, sealed indictment, which translated into nearly 300 years in prison. In addition to a draconian Department of Justice, and facing life behind bars, Henry had to contend with a duplicitous *Washington Post* that was resolute in its reinforcement of the government's cover story. So Henry found himself crushed by the juggernaut of wayward government might and the deception of the media.

The feds initially slapped Henry with 63-months in prison. He thought that if he were mum about the crimes he had witnessed, he would be allowed to live out the balance of his life in relative obscurity, but he eventually discovered that respites for a man who knows too much are a rarity. Affronts from the Justice Department and demonization by media have continued to plague him since his initial incarceration nearly 25 years ago.

I initially spoke to Henry 12 years ago. I was writing a book about the malignant constellation of events that ensnared him, and he was extremely reluctant to talk to me. In fact, it took him two years before he mustered the nerve to give me an interview. I never thought he would muster the nerve to write a tell all book about his life. But in 2012, Henry was in the midst of enduring yet another round of assaults by the government and media, and he was exasperated. He phoned me and said that the time had finally come for him to write a book about his life and illuminate the nefarious matrix of events that had overwhelmed him in Washington, D.C. I was surprised by his decision, because he's assiduously attempted to live his life in anonymity.

Although the latter round of onslaughts by the government and the media incensed Henry, it nonetheless took him months to steel himself to discuss the particulars of his life. And even as we worked on this book, Henry had to contend with government persecution and media assaults. After several stops and starts, we finally completed *Confessions of a D.C. Madam.* In addition to elucidating a spirit that refused to be broken, this book contains shocking and disturbing revelations about the incomprehensible cauldron of corruption that lurks below the surface of American politics.

Nick Bryant 2/22/14

Deborah Jeane Palfrey
R.I.P. 1956-2008

CHAPTER ONE

DÉJÀ VU

I routinely wake between 4:30 A.M. and 5:00 A.M. without the benefit of an alarm clock, and on that particular morning I awoke around 5:00 A.M. I'm self-employed and my businesses are flourishing, so I have the luxury of waking whenever I decide to awake, but nearly eight years of incarceration, courtesy of the federal government, have hardwired me to have an early-to-bed and early-to-rise constitution. I've never been accused of indolence, even though the government and media have branded me as a criminal mastermind of sorts.

After I climbed out of bed, I quietly stepped into the bedroom's walk-in closet and slipped into a light blue sweat suit and running shoes. Before departing the bedroom, I gazed at my partner who was sound asleep on the bed. I descended a flight of stairs and walked through the living room into the kitchen. I generally shun food in the early morning hours, but I usually imbibe a mug of green tea before I start navigating the day. I filled the tea kettle with water and deposited it on the stove. I then peered out the kitchen window into the predawn darkness, ruminating about the upcoming day, until the whistling tea kettle abruptly pierced my reveries. After pouring a mug of scalding water, I plopped a bag of green tea into it and took a few sips of the tea, which gave me a slight sense of invigoration.

I flicked on the basement light and bounced down the stairs. As I surveyed the basement's treadmill, StairMaster, elliptical, and Nautilus, I caught a glimpse of myself in the basement's mirrored walls. Somnolence covered my face like a wilted mask, and incorrigible tufts of blond hair had yet to be tamed by a shower and a brush. I reached for the remote, resting on the treadmill, and I flicked on the television that was mounted on the wall. I gazed upward at CNN as I started trotting on the treadmill. CNN and the treadmill have been a morning ritual I've cultivated since my previous stint in prison.

I had been on the treadmill for about ten minutes, listlessly peering upwards at the television, when the expression "D.C. Madam" sliced through the air. The words jolted me as if they were fired from a stun gun, and I felt momentary paralysis. I was nearly hurled from the treadmill, but I had the wherewithal to leap off the track while I became transfixed on the television. CNN was reporting on the case of Deborah Jeane Palfrey, who ran a Washington, D.C.-based escort service. The media had branded her as the D.C. madam. CNN flashed a picture of Ms. Palfrey: She had shoulder length brunette hair, benign bronze eyes, and a porcelain complexion. She had the appearance of a stylish librarian or high school English teacher, even though the government accused her of being a "racketeer."

The media had branded me a "D.C. madam" years before Deborah Jeane Palfrey was given that distinction. Although the media's reportage on me has been distorted and derisive, it's indeed accurate that at the sprite age of twenty-nine I was the proprietor of the largest gay escort service in Washington, D.C. The Washington Post's skewed coverage of me was due to the fact that the newspaper—by either commission or omission—took its queue from the federal government, which manufactured a labyrinth of lies about my circumstances.

The federal government also unleashed a reign of terror on my family and me. In fact, the feds even threatened to indict my elderly mother, and one newspaper reported that Secret Service agents actually kicked down the front door of my sister's home and held my brother-in-law at gunpoint. The feds felt it was imperative to ensure my silence by any means necessary, because I had witnessed events that invariably would have ignited seismic political cataclysms—political cataclysms that had the potential to jeopardize the administration of George H.W. Bush and the subsequent Bush dynasty.

Given my former incarnation as a D.C. madam, I followed the tribulations, trial, and death of Deborah Jeane Palfrey with intense interest. I marveled at the striking similarities between our cases, and I empathized with her dire circumstances. On *Larry King Live*, Ms. Palfrey dispensed a warning to Americans about their corrupt political system: " ... think about it a bit, and you'll come to the conclusion that we have come to. That there are possible people who have used the service who have become the subjects and targets of blackmail ... "

I'm uncertain if Ms. Palfrey witnessed the blackmailing of politicians first-hand, but I was certainly privy to the blackmailing of politicians and sundry powerbrokers. If the Department of Justice, the Secret Service, and the *Washington Post* had not been fixated on covering up the facts and individuals enmeshed in my case, Americans would have learned the unsavory truth that blackmail is endemic to their political system. The sexual escapades of the D.C. elite are vastly different than the infidelities of the average citizen—thus their susceptibility to blackmail.

Before Ms. Palfrey's trial, she imparted flurries of sound bites to the media intimating that she was the custodian of too many secrets, and the government would be unlocking a Pandora's Box if it prosecuted her. "I am sure as heck am not going to be going to federal prison for one day, let alone, you know, four to eight years here, because I'm shy about bringing in the deputy secretary of whatever," Palfrey told ABC. "Not for a second. I'll bring every last one of them in if necessary."

I, like Ms. Palfrey, thought that the secrets I had amassed over the years would discourage the government from prosecuting me. After the Secret Service's initial raid and ransacking of my home, and prior to being indicted, I remarked to a reporter: "Somebody set us up because they were scared about what we knew about high government officials.... And anyways, if they do try to indict me, I'll have some good stories to tell." I was a mere 29 years old when I dispensed that quote, and, regrettably, I had the aplomb and inexperience of youth, which is an extremely flawed tandem when locking horns with the federal government. I woefully underestimated the ruthlessness and absolute power of my adversary.

Ms. Palfrey followed through on her threat and attempted to unfurl her secrets: She presented ABC News with forty-three pounds of printed pages that contained the phone numbers of the thousands of johns who frequented her escort service over the years. Ms. Palfrey had no idea of the names accompanying the vast majority of the phone numbers, and she hoped that ABC would decipher that information. She felt that the potentially pyrokinetic scoop she handed to ABC would force the government on the defensive and impede its zealous crusade to imprison her.

But her counter-offensive spectacularly backfired: ABC refused to follow through on the revelations contained in the 43-pound printout. ABC correspondent Brian Ross announced that "based on our reporting, it turned out not to be as newsworthy as we thought in terms of the names," even though it would emerge that Palfrey's patrons included, for starters, a U.S. Senator, a Department of Defense consultant who developed the "shock and awe" doctrine deployed on Iraq, and State Department official Randall Tobias. In a stunning demonstration of hypocrisy, Tobias was the Agency for International Development's Director of Foreign Assistance, and he managed agencies that required the foreign recipients of AIDS assistance to condemn prostitution.

The federal government subjected both Ms. Palfrey and me to crucible that was designed to ensure our silence—or ultimately crush us. "They just destroy you on every level—financially, emotionally, psychologically," Ms. Palfrey reportedly said of federal prosecutors. In the case of Ms. Palfrey, the U.S. Attorney for the District of D.C. smacked her with a 14-count RICO indictment that included money laundering, racketeering, and using the mail for illegal purposes in connection with a prostitution ring, and she was facing a bewildering fifty-five years behind bars. RICO is an acronym for the Racketeer Influenced and Corrupt Organizations Act, and it was originally designed to dismantle the Mafia, as RICO allows for mob bosses to be tried for crimes that were sanctioned on their behalf. Ms. Palfrey was merely running an escort service, so it seems that the RICO Act was prosecutorial overkill in her circumstances—unless, of course, prosecutors felt it was imperative to leverage her silence.

I, too, was merely running an escort service, but the U.S. Attorney for the District of D.C. walloped me with a 43-count RICO indictment. I was potentially staring at 295 years behind bars! I was also looking at the possibility of a two million dollar fine, and, as I've previously mentioned, the feds were threatening to indict my mother.

Although my case and Ms. Palfrey's share numerous parallels, a major point of divergence is the proficiency of our respective attorneys. D.C.-based attorney Montgomery Sibley represented Ms. Palfrey and Greta Van Susteren represented me. Mr. Sibley vigorously defended Ms. Palfrey, but he had to contend with the feds judicial chicanery and sleight-of-hand. Ms. Palfrey's initial trial judge had authorized Mr. Sibley's subpoenas of the White House, State Department, CIA, etc., and he also authorized subpoenas for AT&T Mobility, Sprint/Nextel, T-Mobile USA, and Alltel, which would have mandated those carriers to provide Ms. Palfrey with the names and addresses of the individuals who contacted her escort service. Inexplicably, Ms. Palfrey's initial trial judge was replaced by a judge who quashed Mr. Sibley's subpoenas en masse, and thereby eviscerated the defense's case.

At the outset of my case, my attorney, Greta Van Susteren, seemed very committed to a vigorous defense on my behalf, and she deployed a nearly identical tactic as Mr. Sibley—she filed an eleven-page motion to mandate the release of my clientele list that the government had previously seized from me. Ms. Van Susteren argued that the names of my patrons should be released, because, if the government's assertion was accurate and my "escort" service was, in actuality, a prostitution ring, my clients aided and abetted a criminal enterprise.

But the Assistant U.S. Attorney for D.C. vehemently contested Ms. Van Susteren's motion with a remarkably disingenuous argument: He contended that the names of my patrons shouldn't be made public, because the U.S. Attorney's office feared the "intimidation of government witnesses due to the embarrassing nature of the case." My trial judge sided with the prosecution and barred the public disclosure of my clientele. After my trial judge acquiesced to the U.S. Attorney's office, Ms. Van Susteren started to change her tune, and she urged me to take the government's plea bargain.

By then, my family and I had been subjected to a relentless campaign of terror, and I faced life in prison—I felt as if the feds were wielding the Sword of Damocles over my head. At Ms. Van Susteren's behest, I accepted the government's plea bargain, and I was sentenced to 63 months in federal prison. The feds also included a caveat that wasn't overtly stated in my plea agreement: My 5-year sentence was based on the contingency that I not divulge a word about the particulars of my case to the media.

Although I'm uncertain whether or not it's a mere coincidence, I should point out that the individuals who were instrumental in the cover up of my case experienced significant upward mobility: Ms. Van Susteren now has her very own television show on FOX, and the U.S. Attorney for the District of D.C., who imprisoned me and ensured my silence, is now a Vice President of the Raytheon Corporation, one of the world's largest defense contactors.

After I was gagged and banished to a federal prison, I've been told that the government sealed, in perpetuity, a myraid of documents in my case. I'm aware of at least three individuals who have attempted to unseal my documentation, but the government has successfully rebuffed each of them.

Conversely, Ms. Palfrey opted to fight City Hall, but the U.S. Attorney for D.C. triumphed in her case, and she was found guilty on all counts. As Ms. Palfrey awaited sentencing, she purportedly committed suicide. Ms. Palfrey's death is mired in conjecture, rumor, and innuendo, and the Internet is rife with speculation that Ms. Palfrey's suicide was indeed a murder.

Ms. Palfrey publicly stated on a handful of occasions that she would never commit suicide, which buttresses the contentions that she was murdered. Moreover, after Ms. Palfrey's demise, an Orlando affiliate of CBS interviewed the building manager of the Park Lake Towers in Orlando, where Ms. Palfrey owned a condo. The building manager disclosed that he had talked to Ms. Palfrey just three days before her lifeless body was found in her mother's aluminum shed. "Jeane Palfrey was a class act," said the building manager. "Her way out of this world certainly would not have been in an aluminum shed attached to a mobile home in Tarpon Springs, Florida." The manager also discussed a disturbing conversation he had with Ms. Palfrey: "She insinuated that there is a contract out for her, and I fully believe they succeeded."

The *Washington Post* was quick to declare that Palfrey had taken her own life—despite the possibility of indications to the contrary. I mention the latter point because the *Washington Post* reported a myriad of details about my case that were inaccurate—despite the possibility of indications to the contrary—or solely based on the word of federal law enforcement officials. Although I'm unwilling to speculate whether or not the death of Ms. Palfrey was a suicide or a murder, I feared for my life when I was a D.C. madam due to the threats discharged by government officials and also by individuals who were reportedly affiliated with the government.

As Ms. Palfrey and I regrettably discovered, Americans have a collective naiveté about D.C. sex scandals, believing that they are the mere dalliances and moral failings of a handful of individuals. Americans have great difficulty accepting that many of our politicians are endowed with a potent alchemy of power, arrogance, and lust—an alchemy that fluently translates into extramarital affairs or illicit sexual encounters. Unfortunately, the federal government has a greater dexterity to cover up scandals and crimes that lend themselves to blackmail in D.C. due to the fact that the capital's law enforcement is exclusively controlled by various branches of the federal government: The U.S. Attorney for D.C., who prosecutes all D.C. crimes, is appointed by the president. The FBI and Secret Service are also minions of the executive branch, and Congress controls the budget of D.C.'s Metropolitan Police Department.

I would be remiss if I didn't mention that the D.C. press corps played an integral role in the cover up surrounding my case. I've already alluded to the fact that the *Washington Post* aided and abetted the cover up of my case by tainting its reportage with the government's top-spin, but the *Washington Post* was by no means the only media outlet that covered up the factual circumstances of my case: Perhaps a number of the high-flyers in the D.C. press corps aren't mindful of the blackmail that has usurped the American political process, but I'm also aware of nationally recognized pundits who are potentially compromised themselves—because they were patrons of my escort service.

I initially thought that if I adhered to the Faustian pact I made with the government and remained mute about the feds' labyrinth of lies and served my time, I would be permitted to live out the balance of my life in peace, but the government and media have continued to persecute me. Bloggers on the Internet have also taken their queue from the government and the media, and the Internet is rife with lies about me too.

Although I've transformed myself into a legitimate and very successful businessman, and I am a poster boy for a reformed felon, I've been inexorably stalked by a wayward federal judiciary, and a pernicious 20-year assault on my character. Consequently, I have finally decided to rupture my silence and expose the illicit skullduggery I witnessed as a D.C. madam, and also the Byzantine machinations that the government fabricated to ensure my silence and incarcerate me.

CHAPTER TWO

COUNTRY ROADS

Twenty-nine years before I was christened the "D.C. madam," I was born in South Williamson, Kentucky, at the Appalachian Regional Hospital on November 27, 1960. My parents, Charles and Joyce Vinson, lived in Nolan, West Virginia, a tiny hamlet nestled in a remote southwest corner of the state. Nolan was built along the banks of the meandering Tug Fork River, which divides West Virginia's Mingo County and Kentucky's Pike County. Topographically, downtown Nolan was a linear spattering of two-dozen buildings that were wedged among besieging poplars, sugar maples, red maples, white oaks, and red oaks. Like scores of towns sprinkled throughout the rolling and dense woodlands of West Virginia, Nolan emerged because of the booming coal industry of the 1800s and 1900s. The Norfolk and Western Railway cuts right through Nolan, and thundering trains, laden with coal, were a constant presence in my childhood.

Of the thousands of cities and towns scattered throughout the United States, Nolan, West Virginia, seems an improbable candidate to nurture a D.C. madam. Nolan, after all, is in the heart of Appalachia, and the Tug Fork River was the legendary divide between the feuding Hatfields and McCoys. Growing up gay in Appalachia in the 1960s was like being banished to one of the inner circles of Dante's inferno. Pop culture has eschewed the theme of homosexuality in Appalachia except for the film *Deliverance*, which isn't a very encouraging depiction.

My parents met in high school, and they married at the age of seventeen. I was their third and last child. My father, Charles, had five siblings, and the Vinsons were an unruly clan that largely consisted of drunkards and scoundrels. I have a tendency to suspect that many of the Vinson men were endowed with an extra Y chromosome. My paternal great grandfather had been a legendary bootlegger and moonshiner, and my paternal grandfather, Walter, and his brothers inherited his ill begotten largesse. The vestiges of my great grandfather's spoils trickled down to my father and his brothers.

Walter was tall, lean, and he had a thick thatch of unruly black hair that was parted to the right. A life of fighting, drink, and infidelity had carved premature grooves and furrows on his swarthy face, and he had a reputation for being vicious. One of my aunts once stabbed him in the stomach with a knife during a drunken fracas, and then she dutifully drove him to the hospital to be stitched up. Of course, by the time they arrived at the hospital, the deep gash on my grandfather's belly had been amended to a mere "accident."

In contrast, my mother's family was deeply religious, and they were devoted churchgoers. My maternal grandfather was a Baptist preacher on Sunday, and a life insurance salesman Monday through Saturday. He was quite industrious, as he insured his flock for not only this world, but also for the hereafter. My maternal grandfather died of a heart attack before I was born, and he was survived by his wife, Bessie Mae, and seven children—my mother, her two sisters, and four brothers. Unlike my father's siblings, most of mother's brothers and sisters fled West Virginia at their first opportunity. My mother's four brothers enlisted in the Army or Marines as teenagers.

My father and mother married in 1950, and they settled into a green, two-story house near Route 52, a two-lane "highway" that was the main thoroughfare skirting the fringes of West Virginia when I was growing up. My parents rickety house was furbished with a minimalistic interior decorating style that was popular in Appalachia circa 1950—second-hand, threadbare furniture. Our house was on a hill overlooking the Tug Fork River and the north end of Nolan, and it offered a view of the toll bridge crossing the Tug Fork River into Kentucky and the railroad yard's handful of Norfolk and Western

Railway's cinderblock buildings. The railroad yard was always a beehive of activity.

My brother, Charles Walter Vinson, Jr., was born in 1951. It had been a foregone conclusion that my brother would be my father's namesake, but he quickly acquired the nickname of Butch. My brother inherited the tall, dark, and handsome features of the Vinsons, and the thoughtful and considerate personality of my mother's family. Butch was athletic and popular in school, and the girls flocked to him.

My sister, Brenda, was born a year after Butch. She was short and overweight. She had brown hair, brown eyes, and a plump face. Whereas my brother was outgoing and personable, my sister was withdrawn and pensive. I came on the scene about eight years after my sister. I was short, bashful, and overly sensitive with blue eyes and blond hair. My appearance was markedly different than my sister and brother, so, even as a child, I felt out of place in the Vinson household. My father often belted out that I didn't belong in his family, and my earliest memories of the Vinson household are not particularly favorable.

My father and two of his brothers had the mineral rights to a tract of land thirty miles west of Nolan in Kentucky, and, after a day of coal mining, it wasn't uncommon for him to come home in the evening. His flannel shirt and dungarees would be caked by dirt and soot. His taut face had the razor sharp contours that were the product of a life whetted by rage. He would fester in silence as he poured out a tumbler of vodka. He would then sink into the living room's green couch, watch TV, preferably professional wrestling, and start swilling vodka.

After he took his first slug of vodka, his brows would furrow, and his lips would purse. As he became increasing intoxicated, his silent festering would yield to racist rants and hollering at my mother and siblings. In fact, it wasn't uncommon for him to haul off and punch my mother or brother. By the time of my birth, my siblings had learned that their emotional and physical wellbeing dictated that they make themselves scarce when my father was in the house. It was a lesson that I would quickly learn too.

My first dog, Brownie, was not only my first friend, but taking him outside to play offered me a safety outlet to escape my father. Brownie was a mutt of the Heinz 57 variety—he had liver coloring and patches of white around his face. Brownie would be the first of my three dogs that met a premature death on Route 52. When my mother broke the news to me that a truck had hit Brownie, I cried every day for weeks.

Brownie's demise was my childhood's initial lesson on the impermanence of life, and, as I look back on my life, my childhood was certainly drenched in death. My father had a rather morbid pastime of spending hours listening to a police scanner, and then piling my mother and me into his red pick up truck to ogle the scene of a fatal accident. My brother and sister were spared from this morbid pastime, but my mother grudgingly accompanied him to maintain the peace.

My father's forays to the sites of accidents would often be our Saturday night entertainment, and the next morning my mother and I would invariably attend Nolan Freewill Baptist Church. My father and brother never attended Sunday services, and my sister would occasionally accompany us. Nolan Freewill Baptist Church was a single-story, cinderblock building with a pitched roof. The small church accommodated about fifty congregants, sitting in eight rows of wooden pews, and Pastor Ray Taylor was always at the pulpit. Pastor Taylor was short and stout, and he had thinning white hair, frosty blue eyes, and a spherical face. Pastor Taylor sported blue suits, white shirts, and gray ties.

If I described Pastor Taylor as a "preacher," it would almost be a misnomer—he was a screamer. He was a staccato whirlwind of gesticulations as he shouted the "word" at the congregation. Pastor Taylor looked as if he were in the midst of an epileptic seizure during his sermons except for the fact that he would often and methodically wipe the sweat from his brow and forehead with a white handkerchief. His zeal was like a current of electricity nettling the congregation, and they would throw their hands into the air and start speaking in tongues. I found Nolan Freewill Baptist Church to be utterly confusing, and the services could last for two or three hours. I envied my father and brother insofar as they were spared from attending Sunday services.

My maternal grandmother, Bessie Mae, was an avid church-goer, but she emanated a rarefied love and compassion that I felt was lacking in the lives of many of the church's parishioners. She lived a few blocks from us, so I quickly learned to take refuge at her house to flee the tyranny of my father. I visited her almost every day. She was 5'6", heavy set, and she had a round, fleshy face. Her gray hair was always tucked into a bun, and she wore black-framed glasses. She had the appearance of an archetypical grandmother, and I was closer to her than I was to my brother and sister.

Granma Bessie Mae and I would periodically hop into her white Volkswagen beetle and drive east on Route 52 for ten miles to the great metropolis of Williamson, West Virginia, which had a population of around 8,000 denizens. As a little boy, I was overwhelmed and frightened by Williamson's swell of people walking on the sidewalks and the cars skirting up and down paved streets—Main Street and Nolan Street were the only paved streets in Nolan.

Our sojourns into Williamson would be punctuated by a visit to D.C. Murphy, a five-and-dime store with a soda counter. After Bessie May bought me a malted milkshake at the counter, we would peruse the store's aquariums that held a variety of fish—I was particularly attracted to the goldfish. Granma Bessie Mae also cleaned Nolan Elementary School at night, and my mother and I often gave her a hand. I remember running through the hallways of the school as if imaginary villains were chasing me.

I also avoided my father by wandering over to Uncle Oliver's store, J.R. Vinson Grocery, which was a half block from our house. Uncle Oliver's store was an unpainted cinderblock building that had two front windows, and each window had "J.R. Vinson Grocery" in black lettering. The store's glass paneled front door required a skeleton key. Two counters, to the left and right of the front door, stretched the length of the small store. The counter to the left accommodated a cash register and a glass-encased candy rack. Shelves steeped with canned foods were behind the counter to the right. A cooler brimming with bottles of soda and milk was in the back.

Uncle Oliver had the swarthy features of the Vinsons, but he was taller than my father, and he also had a hefty paunch. He usually wore plaid shirts, black pants, and black shoes. He had a hunched-over physique as he leisurely shuffled around the store. A Camel straight perpetually dangled from his mouth. Uncle Oliver's store primarily catered to the impoverished of Nolan, who needed credit to make ends meet from paycheck to paycheck, so he had a large "credit rack" that rested next to the cash register. Whenever he wrote a credit slip, he would set his cigarette on the edge of the counter and wet the pencil tip in his mouth.

Uncle Oliver had a personality that was more jocular than his brothers, but he didn't escape the Vinson curse—drink—and he often called on me to be his gofer. Two or three times a week, I would walk into Nolan, traverse the railroad tracks, and pick up a quart or two of Falls City beer for him at his favorite tavern. When I initially made the beer runs for Uncle Oliver, the trains terrified me. I stood at the railroad crossing awed by trembling ground and the massive locomotive barreling towards me. As the locomotive thundered by me and blasted its deafening horn, my heart pounded against my chest like a jackhammer. The scent of diesel fuel also lingered in the air.

•••

At the age of six, I started attending Nolan Elementary School. The school was a three-story cinderblock building, and each grade huddled into a single classroom. My first grade classroom had green walls, unfinished wood floors, and a single window. The dark, dingy room accommodated about forty kids.

My first grade teacher, Mrs. Reed, was short and overweight. She had an alabaster face, and a thick mane of black hair. Mrs. Reed looked like she applied her mottled makeup with a trowel, and she wore very bright, red lipstick, which imparted the facial appearance of a circus clown. Mrs. Reed was kind and warm-hearted, but she occasionally remarked that I was "too pretty to be a boy." Although she didn't dispense her remarks with malice, they subconsciously cut like a dagger, even though I had absolutely no awareness of my homosexuality.

Mr. Chapman, the principal, was in his mid-fifties, and his pasty white skin was generously sprinkled with freckles. He had thinning gray hair, and a pair of wire-rimmed glasses rested snugly on his stern face. Mr. Chapman was a strict disciplinarian, and he once paddled me for talking in class. He unleashed such a furious flurry of paddles on my rump that it dissuaded me from ever talking in class again.

Mr. Chapman also had a rather unusual foible that would ultimately alter the trajectory of my life. Nolan Grade School neighbored Nolan Freewill Baptist Church, and Mr. Chapman had an aversion to memorial services at the church that were sparsely attended. If a memorial service at the church had a shortage of mourners, he would march students into the church, single-file, to fill the vacant pews. So, as a child, I sat through numerous services.

M.T. Ball was the funeral director who oversaw the majority of the memorial services. The Ball Funeral Home was located in Williamson, and Mr. Ball was a tall, slender older man who wore impeccable three-piece suits. In addition to being meticulous about his appearance, he was exceptionally soft spoken, polite, and courteous. His mannerisms were gentle and benign, and he had the mental dexterity to stop whatever task he was undertaking and give grieving families his undivided attention. Mr. Ball made bereaved families feel like they were truly the most important people in the world as he comforted them like a warm salve. I had never met anyone quite like M.T. Ball, and the process of death started to fascinate me.

•••

All of the first grade boys seemed to wear beige khakis or blue jeans, sweatshirts, and tennis shoes, which I also wore. But I had the unsettling sense that I was markedly different than my classmates. I felt as if they had been given a manual on the conventions and mores of being a first grader, and I had been passed over for the manual. I think that the alienation I felt from my classmates was the estrangement I felt in my family seeping into classroom.

Luckily, I quickly befriended a couple of classmates who also seemed to experience the estrangement that plagued me—Danny and Kevin. Danny was overweight and a little shorter than me, and he had thick, wavy dark brown hair. He was very quiet and shy, but he was extremely smart. Kevin had straight, light brown hair, and he was thin as a rail. We lived fairly close to each other, so we walked to and from school everyday.

Danny, Kevin and I played marbles and hopscotch during recess. After school, we would walk for hours along the railroad tracks or follow the banks of the Tug Fork River. As we wandered through dense mosaics of poplar trees that seemed to touch the clouds, we thought we were "exploring" wilderness that had yet to be treaded by mankind.

It was always an adventure to dash across the Tug Fork River railroad bridge that connected West Virginia and Kentucky. Years later, when I watched the movie *Stand By Me*, I thought it captured the exhilaration we experienced sprinting across the bridge. We periodically wandered up to a cemetery that was on the outskirts of Nolan. We were always terrified when we tottered around the old cemetery, because, at any given moment, we expected dead bodies to suddenly arise from their graves like zombies and give chase.

First grade would ultimately be a devastating lesson on life's impermanence: Danny and Kevin died within four months of each other. An aggressive brain cancer abruptly purloined Danny's life, and a speeding car struck Kevin. Their memorial services were held at Nolan Freewill Baptist Church, and Pastor Taylor delivered both eulogies as he stood over their tiny, glistening caskets.

As Pastor Taylor howled about heaven and hell, I felt as if I were underwater, so his words were almost inaudible to me. M.T. Ball was the funeral director for both services, and his compassionate smile and thoughtful words seemed to assuage my grief considerably more than Pastor Taylor's eulogy or my mother's insistence that both boys were destined for heaven.

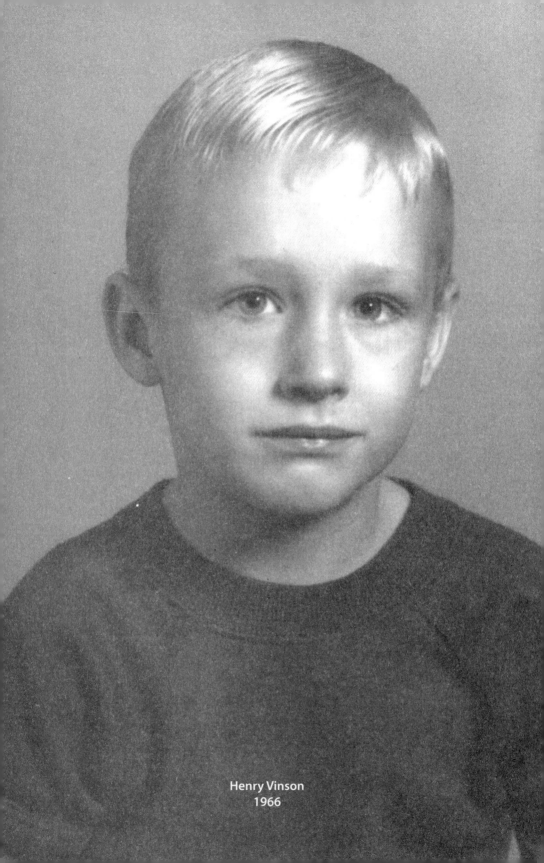

Henry Vinson
1966

CHAPTER THREE

SONGS OF INNOCENCE

Shortly after Kevin's funeral, I became extremely forlorn, and I wandered over to Uncle Oliver's store. Aunt Flora, Uncle Oliver's wife, was attending to a handful of baby pigs that had been delivered to the store. Aunt Flora was slim, and she was fond of long, pastel flowered dresses. She also wore a dark brown, shoulder-length wig. Aunt Flora was very sharp and articulate, and she had a fundamentally different personality than Uncle Oliver. Although she also attended Nolan Freewill Baptist Church, she was the town gossip.

Aunt Flora noticed that I quickly fell in love with one of the baby pigs. He had a bright pink face, light pink skin, very fine body hair, and a tiny curled up tail. She handed him to me like he was a pup, and I cradled him as I walked home. I named him Arnold. Initially, I deposited Arnold in a small cardboard box right next to my bed, and I fed him milk from a baby bottle. During the day, he followed me everywhere. Arnold quickly became not only my favorite pet, but also my best friend. He had a wonderful personality.

Arnold quickly grew to be the size of a small dog, and I fed him table scraps and carrots—Arnold loved carrots. He also relished popcorn. He was extremely smart and affectionate. Indeed, he was far brighter than my dogs, and he was quite easy to potty train. I eventually kept him in a cage in the basement. Whenever Arnold heard me descending the basement stairs, he squealed and his little tail wiggled. When I let him out of his cage, he immediately rolled over on his back—Arnold loved to have his belly rubbed. As Arnold started growing into an adult hog, my mother conscripted my brother build a pen for him in the backyard. I regularly bathed Arnold with the backyard hose, but it was usually to no avail, because he reveled rolling around in the mud. After I gave Arnold a bath, I straddled his back, and he would literally give me piggyback rides around the yard.

Around the time Aunt Flora gave me Arnold, my mother bought me a used upright piano, and she drove me to weekly piano lessons in Williamson in her green Ford Galaxy 500. My piano was in the basement between a chalkboard and Arnold's cage.

I had great difficulty making new friends in school after Danny and Kevin died, so the basement quickly became my imaginary kingdom. I practiced the piano four or five hours a day with Arnold curled up at my feet. I also spent hours sketching on the chalkboard and reading books. If I played the piano softly, my father wouldn't complain about the "noise," and he would leave me alone. I loved playing the Carpenters' music, but I also practiced gospel music, because I frequently played the piano at Nolan Freewill Baptist Church.

Our house overlooked the Nolan Toll Bridge, and I was inexplicably spellbound by it. At the age of seven, I summoned the courage to venture to Nolan Toll Bridge. The tollbooth collector, Erna Mae, was a portly woman in her mid-fifties, which seemed ancient to me. She was deeply religious, and she wouldn't touch makeup. Erna Mae unvaryingly wore loose fitting, long-sleeved housedresses that draped her ankles. Her long, grayish black hair was tucked into a bun, and a pair of black-framed, coke-bottle glasses magnified her gentle brown eyes. Erna Mae's husband was the preacher at the Christ Only Church, where my paternal grandmother, Ada, was a parishioner, so she recognized me even before I introduced myself.

Erna Mae would eventually develop unyielding compassion and love for me, as if she were my grandmother, but the Christ Only Church she attended with my grandmother Ada scared the living daylights out of me. The preachers at the church handled poisonous snakes as they expounded the "word." Snake handling preachers aren't uncommon in Appalachia due to their literal interpretation of a passage from the *Gospel of Mark*: "And these signs will follow those who believe: in My name they will cast out demons; they will speak with new tongues; they will take up serpents; and if they drink anything deadly, it will by no means hurt them; they will lay their hands on the sick, and they will recover." I snuck up to the entrance of the Christ Only Church during three or four services, but I never had the nerve to wander inside.

Starting in second grade, I began a ritual that lasted for years. After school, I would walk to Granma Ada's house, and she would serve me a biscuit with homemade syrup. I then walked over to Nolan Toll Bridge and spent a couple of hours talking to Erna Mae as she collected tolls. The elevated tollbooth had a large glass window, so I could see the trains speeding through Nolan, and also the faces of everyone who stopped to pay their toll.

I was mesmerized by the tollbooth's gleaming, metallic blue cash register—it was a Class 24 Model from National Cash Register—and I thought it was the most amazing machine in the world. A year or so after I made my initial trek to Nolan Toll Bridge, Erna Mae started to let me collect tolls. I was elated as I operated the cash register for the first time—I loved pressing its buttons. The tolls were 3¢ per pedestrian and 15¢ per car plus 3¢ per each additional passenger. I loved watching the different people and perusing the sundry items in their cars and trucks. I wondered about their origins and their destinations.

After spending a few hours at Nolan Toll Bridge each day, I walked home and quickly skirted into the basement, where I played with Arnold and practiced the piano. I rarely ventured into the living room to watch television, because I was wary of my father and never quite sure when he might turn up. Besides, the only TV shows I truly liked were Mutual of Omaha's *Wild Kingdom* and *The Lawrence Welk Show,* and my father hated both. If he caught me watching either show, I would be subjected to torrents of his contempt. He often derided me as a "flat-faced sissy." My mother had been hired as a Mingo County school bus driver, and she was never around in the early evening to protect me from my father, so the basement served as my sanctuary in the Vinson home.

Family sit-down dinners in the Vinson household were rarely pleasant. My father's scorn superimposed on a couple tumblers of vodka would detonate into ridicule of my mother, my siblings, or me. My mother, by her own account, was also never fond of cooking; so after she became a school bus driver, we rarely had dinner as a family. Most of the time our evening meals consisted of TV dinners or sandwiches.

But I'll never forget a sit-down family dinner when I was seven. My father started to taunt my brother for his longish hair. My brother initially attempted to ignore him, but my father's taunts escalated into scathing rebukes. Finally, a fistfight ignited between my father and brother. After my mother managed to break up their fight, my brother stormed out of the house. A few days later, Butch dropped out of high school and moved to Columbus, Ohio, where he started to work for one of our cousins who owned a furniture store.

•••

Second grade was tough for me, because I never found friends to fill the void left by Danny and Kevin's death, but a syrup saturated biscuit at Granma Ada's and a few hours at Nolan Toll Bridge with Erna Mae were a welcome diversion from school. In third grade, a gaggle of fifth- and sixth-graders started to bully me. They said I looked like a girl or talked like a girl. They would routinely shove me as I walked down the hallway. At recess, I was especially prone to being bullied, and I quickly learned not to stray too far from our teacher.

Throughout my childhood, my father had frequent rows with his brothers about the operation of their mining venture. The rows often flared into fistfights and my father dispensing death threats to his brothers. When I was nine years old, my father and his brothers at last came to an irreconcilable impasse, and my father became a Mingo County Deputy Sheriff.

My father loved his deputy sheriff uniform. He had my mother perpetually starching and ironing his uniforms, and he spent countless hours over the years spit shining his black shoes. After his uniform was satisfactorily starched and ironed to his lofty standards, and his shoes were adequately shined, he would ceremoniously don his uniform. After tucking in his shirt, he stood in front of the mirror for a minute or so appraising his appearance.

I suspect my father was so scrupulous about his uniform, because it enabled him to pick up women. Womanizing and vodka seemed to be the primary motivations for his existence, and he never had a shortage of girlfriends. In fact, one of them lived about a block from us. When my mother drove me to piano lessons or when I accompanied her on errands, we occasionally spotted my father driving around with one of his girlfriends. My mother never said a word about his womanizing, because, after he became a deputy sheriff, he was rarely around the house, which came as a great relief to her. His absence came as a great relief to me too.

Although my father treasured being a deputy sheriff, his vodka consumption was unaffected, and I think that he was probably more intoxicated than many of the drivers he arrested for driving under the influence. Moreover, the thought of my father carrying a loaded handgun every day was rather unsettling.

In the wake of my father's metamorphosis from coal miner to deputy sheriff, my sister landed a job as a carhop at a drive-in. Beehive hairdos were the rage in the late 1960s, so my sister was incessantly teasing her hair as she played her forty-five records. She would occasionally take me shopping, and buy me rings, watches, and chains. She once bought me a black onyx ring that I reluctantly wore to school to appease her, and I was incessantly teased about it. By the age of nine, I felt like a walking zoo, and the jewelry she bought for me only exacerbated those feelings. My sister's dates also intermittently stopped by the house, and I felt a vague, inexplicable interest in them, even though I wouldn't be fully conscious of my homosexuality for five or six years.

When I was in fourth grade, my father and sister were never around during the day, and my mother worked a split shift as a school bus driver—mornings and afternoons—so she was free in the late mornings and early afternoons. After school, I continued my ritual of visiting Granma Ada, and then strolling over to Nolan Toll Bridge. But periodically I would stop by our house to feed Arnold or undertake a neglected chore, and O.T. Kent would be sitting in our living room, talking to my mother. Mr. Kent was the Mingo County Schools Superintendent. He had flaxen blond hair and sparkling blue eyes. I thought Mr. Kent bore a striking resemblance to Jim Phelps, the *Mission: Impossible* character played by Peter Graves.

Mr. Kent was like the second coming of Santa Claus to me. He showered me with presents—Matchbox cars, Tonka trucks, Erector Sets, etc. He would also dig into his pockets, pull out a wad of bills, peel off a couple of bucks, and suggest that I buy ice cream or candy. In retrospect, it's evident to me that Mr. Kent was quite fond of being alone with my mother. Indeed, I would discover twenty years later that he was, in fact, my biological father.

As my ostensible father became increasingly enmeshed in the persona of a deputy sheriff and also in the lives of his various mistresses, he receded further and further from the lives of my mother, my sister, and me, so my brother started to periodically visit us on the weekends. Butch may have felt a touch of guilt for the scant time he had formerly spent with me, because we spent hours and hours together during his visits, and they were always a wellspring of merriment for me. I envied my brother's outgoing and affable personality—everybody seemed to love him.

Butch had developed an interest in aviation, and when he visited he frequently had remote control, gasoline powered toy airplanes in tow. He would drive me to the Mingo County Airport in Williamson, and we would spend the afternoon flying the toy planes. As my brother maneuvered the planes with the remote control, I felt a state of wonderment and a seed was planted—I aspired to be a pilot. After the toy planes invariably crashed, Butch let me keep their remnants. I amassed a bedroom chock full of demolished toy airplanes.

When Butch was in town, he also took me to the Nolan auction on Saturday nights and to various junk shops around Mingo County. He bought me broken down cash registers, because I had become absolutely enthralled by cash registers. I just loved operating the tollbooth's cash register, and I thought National Cash Register was the greatest company in the world. I spent hours taking apart the inoperable cash registers and fixing them. A cash register has thousands of moving parts that can be very sensitive to temperature and dust, so it's not uncommon for one small gear to "freeze" and render the cash register inoperable. After I fixed a cash register, I would sell it or trade it for two or three broken cash registers.

•••

In the fall of fourth grade, I came home to find Arnold missing from his pen. I questioned my mother and sister about Arnold. They shrugged their shoulders, and replied, "Arnold must've run away." I spent that day and night combing Nolan in search of Arnold, but he was nowhere to be found. Following a night of restless sleep, I went to school, and then I sprinted home to once more search for Arnold. Throughout the day and night, I never managed to find him. That night, I hurled myself on my bed and cried for hours. Inexplicably, I had an intuition that I would never again see Arnold. Years later, I came to the realization that Arnold had ended up as bacon, pork chops, ribs, etc.

I suspect my brother heard about Arnold's fate through the grapevine, because shortly after Arnold went missing, Butch visited us, and he gave me a spider monkey named George—I kept him in a cage in our basement. George was cute, but he wasn't tamed, and he was in the habit of throwing his feces and food around the basement. My mother bought a leash for him, and I attempted to take George on walks and tame him, but he repeatedly bit me. Although George only lasted about a month in our home, I think it's safe to say he evaded Arnold's fate.

The summer between fifth and sixth grade was marked by two momentous occasions. The first was my first airplane flight: Granma Bessie Mae, my mother, and I flew to Texas to visit my mother's oldest brother, Clarence. The flight departed from Huntington, West Virginia. I was extremely nervous as I situated myself into a window seat and buckled my safety belt. My mother sensed my anxiety, and she smiled and gently cupped my hand.

After the plane taxied to the runway, it came to a standstill for a few minutes. When its engines started to roar just prior to take off, my mouth parched and adrenaline coursed through my body like an electrical jolt. As the plane sped down the runway, and its nose surged upwards, I felt the uncomfortable sensation of being pressed against my seat. The plane quickly became airborne, and I let out a deep breath. Peering out the window as the city of Huntington receded among the clouds, I experienced an exhilarating liberation: I momentarily felt unshackled from the angst, isolation, and anguish of my childhood. It was truly a blissful feeling.

After we transferred planes at the Atlanta airport, we flew to San Antonio, where Uncle Clarence was awaiting our arrival. Uncle Clarence had been a lifer in the Army, and he was retired. He was tall and muscular, and he had a square face and a gray crew cut—he also had grayish eyes. The military had left an indelible imprint on him, and he spoke in a deep, authoritative voice, but he was very nice to me.

Uncle Clarence owned a number of Dunkin' Donuts that were scattered throughout San Antonio, and the majority of our visit consisted of driving around to his various stores. Uncle Clarence quickly noticed that I was captivated by the machine filling the éclairs with custard, and he let me operate it as my grandmother and mother looked on. When we flew out of San Antonio, I felt the same sense of liberation I felt when we departed Huntington.

A month or so after we returned from San Antonio, Butch moved back to Nolan. He had been having a long distance romance with a nurse who worked at Appalachian Regional Hospital, and they decided to tie the knot. Butch's wife, Nina, was tall: around 5'10", fair skinned, and she had sandy blonde hair. Nina, too, had a beehive hairdo, and I'll never forget her warm, welcoming smile. After a justice of the peace married Butch and Nina, they moved into the two-story white frame house that was next door to our house. Both my mother and I were elated to have Butch living next door.

•••

Shortly after Butch and Nina moved next door, Chattaroy Junior High School was looming on my horizon like a runaway locomotive, and I was absolutely mortified about the prospect of attending a physical education class or baring myself in a locker room. Both my brother and sister had regaled me with anecdotes about physical education class and locker room pranks at Chattaroy Junior High School. Recess at Nolan Elementary School had become excruciating enough, and I thought I would undoubtedly be taunted and preyed upon in Chattaroy's locker room. I expressed my concerns to my mother, and she enrolled me in Sacred Heart School in Williamson for seventh and eighth grade.

Sacred Heart was a Catholic school about ten miles from Nolan Elementary School, but it seemed to be in a distant universe. The school had been built fifteen years earlier, and it was in pristine condition. The classrooms were twice the size of the rooms at Nolan Elementary School, yet they accommodated half the students. The school's walls were painted off-white, and it had tiled floors. Each room also had a wall of windows that allowed sunlight to pour into the classrooms. The school desks' lacquered veneer retained a sheen that made them look as if they were brand new. An additional perk of Sacred Heart was air conditioning.

The Sisters of Saint Joseph comprised the staff of Sacred Heart. They were very strict and ensured that I wasn't taunted or bullied. Over the course of my two years at Sacred Heart, I found it difficult to form friendships with my classmates, but I slightly bonded with a shy, overweight boy named Chris.

I had never been exposed to a Catholic mass prior to enrolling in Sacred Heart, and its rituals fascinated me. The Catholic mass was vastly different than Nolan Freewill Baptist Church. I had grown accustom to Minister Taylor screaming about "fire and brimstone" ad nauseam, so the priest's soft spoken homily was a pleasant departure. I also liked the fact that the Catholics weren't disposed to speaking in tongues.

Although I attended Sacred Heart, my after school custom of visiting Granma Ada and then the Nolan Toll Bridge was unabated. After collecting tolls with Erna Mae, I would wander over to my brother's house. Butch's driving ambition was to become a pilot, so he took flying lessons during the day, and he also worked the graveyard shift as a coal miner. My brother's life was quickly eclipsed by a newborn too. Consequently, he was usually sleeping when I stopped by his house, but I loved to play with his dog. Frosty had a silvery white head, and my brother had trained him perform a myriad of tricks.

As Butch pursued his dream of becoming a pilot, my mother started to realize her entrepreneurial spirit by opening a convenience store, Quick Mart, on Route 52. Quick Mart was a stand-alone white building with an overhanging black-shingled roof. A modification of the Mingo County liquor laws, permitting convenience stores to peddle beer, inspired Quick Mart. Neighboring Pike County in Kentucky was "dry," so Quick Mart's primary commodity was beer, and my mother quickly had a lucrative little enterprise. The store had several coolers overflowing with beer and soda. In fact, the store had so many coolers that it felt like a furnace in the summertime, even though the air conditioner was running full blast. Naturally, I provided the store's cash register—a Sweda Model 46—and I even worked nights. Working at Quick Mart made me feel like an adult, and I desperately wanted to expedite the process to adulthood. I thought life would become easier.

One day, after spending the previous night at Quick Mart, I was in the living room, talking to my mother, when a couple of older, nondescript men knocked on our front door. As they talked to my mother, they were somber and periodically gazed downward. My mother shattered before my very eyes. She burst into tears and started to scream. Her screams tore through me like shrapnel, and I felt momentarily immobilized. My mother's knees buckled, and she crumbled to floor. She seemingly convulsed as she wailed and sobbed. A mining accident had taken Butch's life.

Butch's Grave

CHAPTER FOUR

COMING OF AGE

Butch's memorial service at Nolan Freewill Baptist Church was overflowing with mourners. Our extended family, Nina's family, and several of Butch's friends and coworkers attended. Everyone was stunned that the life of such a vital, vibrant 22-year-old had been extinguished by a fluke mining accident. The mourners' faces were paralyzed by grief, and their tear-glazed eyes had blank, distant stares. The funeral director was a very nice man, but he didn't have the ameliorating spirit of M.T. Ball, who had a distinct style of assuring distraught mourners that they would emotionally prevail.

I wore my Sunday best to the funeral, and my clothes felt itchy and oppressive. Butch's funeral had the same surreal quality as Danny and Kevin's funeral, because it was inconceivable to me that I would never again see my brother. As Pastor Taylor delivered the eulogy, his words were nearly inaudible, and, once more, I had the feeling of being submerged underwater.

In the days leading up to the funeral, I heard persistent discussions about whether or not Butch was destined for heaven due to the fact that he never attended church and had rejected the piety of our mother. After the service, my mother made a beeline to Pastor Taylor, and she asked him if her son was ordained for heaven. Pastor Taylor replied, "Joyce, I had the sweetest feeling when I stood at the head of his casket." Butch was interred at Mountain View Memory Gardens on a cold, blustery overcast day in October of 1973.

Following Butch's funeral, my mother skidded into an abyss of despair. My father, however, promptly molted his grief, and a week or so after Butch's funeral he was overjoyed, because he had tickets to a professional wrestling extravaganza in Williamson. My mother was shocked that he was even entertaining the idea of attending a professional wrestling bout, and she insisted that he remain at home and mourn the loss of his son. A screaming squabble suddenly erupted between them. My mother swore if my father chose professional wrestling over his family, it would end to their marriage. My father slapped her, and, without hesitation, drove to Williamson.

My mother's free fall into despair was relentless, and she took a six-month leave of absence from bus driving. She also started popping Valiums like they were Tic Tac breath mints, and she spent interminable hours in bed with the curtains drawn. Every afternoon, after I came home from school, she would drive me to Mountain View Memory Gardens, and we would visit Butch's grave. As my mother's grief became a black hole that devoured the joy of everyone around her, I began sleeping at Granma Bessie Mae's house.

A couple of months after Butch's death, my sister married her longtime boyfriend, Ralph Copley. Ralph was tall and lumbering, and he worked for the Norfolk and Western Railway. He had bright red hair and a red beard, and freckles collaged his blanched skin. Ralph was even-tempered, placid, and exceptionally kind to me.

Brenda and Ralph's wedding ceremony was held at our house, and a cousin, who was a minister, performed the ceremony. My mother's inexorable grief, superimposed on the overt strife between my mother and father, yielded a wedding that was far from festive. My brother's wife, Nina, had relocated to her parents' house after Butch's death, so my sister and Ralph moved into their former house.

As my mother started to recover from Butch's death, and our day-after-day pilgrimages to Mountain View Memory Gardens tapered, I recommenced my daily treks to Nolan Toll Bridge after Sacred Heart had adjourned for the day. Erna Mae and the tollbooth were a serene departure from my mother's anguish.

Erna Mae's son, Larry, worked at Nolan Toll Bridge too, and he was also a deacon at the Christ Only Church. He was obese, balding, and in his thirties. Larry's home was near the Nolan Toll Bridge, and one day he requested that I assist him with a few chores around his house. He was the keeper of the Christ Only Church's poisonous snakes, so I wasn't particularly thrilled about stepping foot into his home, but I nonetheless accompanied him. When we walked though Larry's living room, I noticed a wooden crate that had a wire mesh covering. I glanced into the crate, and I caught sight of two snakes.

As I was processing the disconcerting fact that I was in close proximity to a pair of poisonous snakes, Larry suddenly pulled down his pants, and asked me to kiss his penis. I felt petrified by fear, and I froze for a moment or two—I then dashed out of his house. My body was flooded by adrenaline as I ran towards the tollbooth. Erna Mae had been a grandmother, a mother, and a best friend to me, so I instinctively thought that she would comfort me after I conveyed to her the dread I had just experienced. I was a bewildered 13-year-old boy, and, at the time, I was incapable of emotionally deciphering that Erna Mae would have conflicted feelings about her son's actions.

When I approached the tollbooth, Erna Mae immediately noticed my dismay, and she cast a concerned expression at me. I was nearly hyperventilating as I described Larry's attempt to molest me. Her facial expressions were like a slot machine wheel that cycled through alarm, apprehension, apathy, and then suddenly stopped at wrath. Erna Mae grimaced and suddenly erupted in a cold, hostile inflection that seemed utterly unfamiliar to her as she ordered me to walk home. I would never again be welcome at Nolan Toll Bridge. Although my childhood had been rife with betrayal, desolation, and devastation, I think that may have been its most devastating moment, because the innumerable hours I spent at the tollbooth were the fondest memories of my childhood.

In the aftershock of realizing that I was forever banished from the Nolan Toll Bridge, I began working at the Nolan Post Office. Starting at the age of eight, my mother routinely sent me to the post office, which was a couple of blocks from our house, and I befriended Terry Walker who was Nolan's postmaster. Terry weighed at least 350 pounds, and he was in his mid-fifties. His face had a bright red hue that even extended to his bald dome. A pair of black-frame glasses with the thickest lenses imaginable rested on his bulbous nose. Terry's legs had been devoured by polio, so he wore metal leg braces and used two canes to amble around the post office. He had diabetes too. Terry and his sister never married, and they lived in the two-story frame house where they grew up next door to the post office.

On weekday afternoons after school and on Saturday mornings, I sorted mail for Terry, and he also sent me on frequent odd jobs and errands. My salary was $25 a week. Despite Terry's ailments and his physical appearance, he was a very sweet man. He had an omnipresent grin on his face, and he was unceasingly cracking jokes. I didn't find his jokes to be particularly humorous, but every time he tossed out a punch line he exploded with a booming guffaw. Terry impressed me by the fact that he seemed to be quite contented with his life, even though fate had dealt him several setbacks. As life has dealt me major adversities and cataclysms, I've struggled to embrace his buoyant attitude in the face of hardship.

As eighth grade at Sacred Heart was culminating, my mother divorced my father. Their caricature of a marriage had essentially unraveled shortly after my brother's death. Butch's passing triggered a profound crisis of faith for my mother: She had stopped attending church every Sunday, and the faith that enabled her to endure my father's antics evaporated. Granma Bessie Mae gave my mother a parcel of land on the periphery of Nolan, and she had a single-story brick house built on it. I felt a tremendous sense of relief as my father's specter faded from my life.

My relief, however, would have a short half-life, because, at the age of fourteen, I started attending Williamson High School as a freshman, and it would be four years of pure, unadulterated hell. The first day I stepped into the locker room for physical education class my worst nightmares were quickly realized. Three freshman whom I had never seen before knotted around me; malice was engraved on their faces. One pushed me into the lockers and snickered, "You should be in the girls' locker room."

After school that first day, I pleaded with my mother to unshackle me from physical education class. She called in a few of the markers she had accrued as a school bus driver, and I was able to forgo physical education class in lieu of study hall.

As a freshman, I was repeatedly called a "faggot" and "queer," and during class I would be subjected to barrages of spitballs. I quickly discovered that I was especially vulnerable to being beaten up and bullied in the bathroom, so I absolutely avoided the bathroom during the break between classes. I would use the bathroom only when I was excused during a class.

Although it was in vogue to ridicule me at Williamson High School, two of my fellow freshmen, Jimmy and Rod, took considerable glee in my torment. Jimmy was short and chubby, and Rod was tall, slender, and handsome. Jimmy's father owned a grocery store in Williamson, and he wore stylish clothes that included a seemingly endless array of Polo shirts. Despite Jimmy's dapper exterior, he had a molten rage roiling inside of him. I'll never understand if it was nature or nurture or, perhaps, both that filled Jimmy with such hatred.

A month or so into my freshman year, I wandered into the bathroom after school had been adjourned for the day, so I presumed I would be safe. But Jimmy and Rod suddenly bounded into the bathroom and blocked the door. They roughed me up, and Jimmy said, "I know you want me." As they paused to laugh and admire their handiwork, I bolted out of bathroom. After that experience, I would only use the bathrooms in an adjacent building that housed the school's administrative offices.

Despite feeling like an utter outcast at Williamson High School, I mustered the pluck to sign up for the school band in my freshman year. Although my forte was the piano, I had also learned to play the trumpet and the band needed trumpet players. In addition to being taunted by the boys in the band, the band director, who also coached various sports, ridiculed me too. After he started to habitually call me a "sissy," I quit the band.

At Williamson High, I ultimately befriended two popular girls named Peggy and Joyce, and they became my improbable guardians. Peggy and Joyce were extremely beautiful, and they were the school's heartthrobs. Peggy was a beautiful brunette who had a perfect body, and Joyce had the long red hair and flawless facial features of a stunning Irish belle. Both Peggy and Joyce were extremely assertive, and guys acquiesced to their wishes like trained poodles.

Peggy and Joyce were the only students who allowed me to sit next to them on the bus, and they always sat at the very back. So, after school, I would dart to the rear of the bus to sit with them. I also sat next to Peggy and Joyce during lunch.

Peggy's father owned a popular bar, and it seemed to me like she was acquainted with everyone at the school. Prior to my friendship with Peggy, I couldn't walk to my locker without being terrorized. But shortly after I befriended Peggy and Joyce, a couple of kids were tormenting me while I was opening my locker, and Peggy hollered: "Leave him alone!" The kids immediately recoiled and left me in peace.

Because high school was so difficult for me, I was an average student. My favorite teacher was Mrs. Gentile, and she taught my favorite class—typing. I excelled at typing tests for speed and accuracy, and also at the 10-key adding machine. My marks for the typing and the adding machine were unparalleled.

When I was fifteen, I belatedly came to the realization that I was gay. I say belatedly, because it was quite evident to everyone else around me. The primary reason I locked away my homosexuality in the distant recesses of my mind is that every Sunday morning since my earliest memories it had been emphatically declared that homosexuality was unequivocally evil and every homosexual had a one-way, non-stop ticket to hell. My father's credo, which was nearly indistinguishable from that of the Ku Klux Klan, also deemed homosexuals to be the most malignant form of life on the planet. Although I had become extremely incredulous of the beliefs expounded by Nolan Freewill Baptist Church and my father, their opinions regarding homosexuality had nonetheless left an indelible blueprint on my young psyche.

After a two-week emotional tug of war, I decided to divulge my homosexuality to my mother, and it took me an additional two days to summon the courage to broach the subject with her.

She was sitting at the dining room table when I approached her. I felt steeped in anxiety as I repeatedly cleared my throat and finally said, "Mom, I need to tell you something about me—" She cut me off with a wave of her hand and replied, "I already know everything there is to know about you."

In my sophomore year, southwest Virginia was pounded by a merciless storm. The Tug Fork River Valley had flooded 36 times throughout the 20th century, but the flood of 1977 was without equal. Water surged over the banks of the river, and it submerged almost of all Nolan, Williamson, and most of the surrounding communities. Houses and stores were ripped from their foundations, bridges crumbled, and cars were swept away. We had no electricity for a couple of weeks, and school was suspended for about a month. Although our house was untouched by the flood, its wake of destruction was breathtaking.

•••

At the age of sixteen, I landed a driver's license, which offered me a newfound freedom. My high school years had been devoid of the "normal" pursuits of my peers—such as parties, Friday nights at the high school football game, dating, etc.—and that trend continued even after I had a driver's license. If I had a few hours to spare, and my mother didn't need her Galaxy 500, I would visit the Johnson Funeral Home, which was about 30 miles from our house.

The proprietor of the Johnson Funeral Home was Fred Johnson, and I met him via Granma Bessie Mae—she had been acquainted with Mr. Johnson for many years. When I lived with Granma Bessie Mae during my mother's meltdown after my brother's death, I confided to her that I aspired to become a funeral director. As a student at Nolan Elementary School, I had been awestruck by the love and compassion M.T. Ball had imparted to mourning families. I yearned to impart that same love and compassion to the bereaved.

On my maiden visit to the Johnson Funeral Home, I remember being saturated by anxiety, because I felt my visit to the funeral home was a vital leap in actualizing my dream. As I drove west on Route 44, I noticed a large brick building that had a yellow sign: JOHNSON FUNERAL HOME. The building housed two storefronts: The Johnson Funeral Home and a beauty shop owned by Fred Johnson's daughter. I parked next to two black Chevrolet Impala station wagons. The Impalas had black, plastic mesh screens on their side windows, and a pair of red lights atop their roofs. Until the late-1970s, funeral homes in West Virginia often moonlighted as ambulance services, so hearses doubled as ambulances.

I cautiously entered the funeral home and slowly wandered down a hallway—an office was to my left and a chapel was to my right. After walking into the office, I suddenly stood before a woman who was sitting behind a desk, smoking a cigarette. She had brown hair and wore a mauve colored dress—she was in her late fifties. I think she sensed my nervousness, because she gave me a gracious greeting in the gravely voice of chain smoker as she directed me to take a seat in front of her desk.

After I sat down, an uncomfortable silence ensued until Fred Johnson burst into the room. He had dishwater blond hair and a beaming, almost cantankerous smile. He stood a slender 6'2" and sported a navy blue, three-piece suit. He thrust out a big paw and firmly shook my hand as he introduced himself. Mr. Johnson was in his late fifties, and I thought that the receptionist was his wife, but she was, in fact, his mother-in-law—his wife was about twenty years younger than him.

Mr. Johnson was jovial and animated while he gave me a tour of the funeral home. He seemed to be lodged in a state of perpetual adolescence. After he showed me the chapel, we walked to the end of the hallway, bypassing a couple of rooms on our left, to a pair of large double doors. Behind the double doors was a vast storage room with twenty-foot ceilings. The storage room was jam-packed with coffins, funeral equipment, signs, etc., and I found it to be rather eerie. Mr. Johnson had an "embalming room" built in a corner of the storage room.

I quickly found myself juggling school, working at my mother's store and the post office, and volunteering at the Johnson Funeral Home. I managed to smuggle the majority of my spare time into volunteering at the funeral home, because I genuinely enjoyed its atmosphere and Mr. Johnson. I initially washed the hearses and performed various janitorial duties. The storage room was cluttered and chaotic, and I attempted to introduce order to it.

Surprisingly, the Johnson Funeral Home didn't have a public restroom, and its only restroom was tucked into a corner of the storage room. The restroom was also cluttered with funeral equipment and jumbles of junk. After using the restroom, I remember a funeral goer remarking to Mr. Johnson, "I wouldn't let you bury my dog in this place," and Mr. Johnson replied, "That's all right—I don't bury dogs."

I eventually started to assist Mr. Johnson with the removal of cadavers from homes and hospitals and embalming. The first time I assisted him with embalming was Thanksgiving Day 1976. After arriving at the funeral home, I accompanied Mr. Johnson to the embalming room. A heavyset, bearded man in his mid-thirties was splayed out on the stainless steel embalming table. He had been shot in the neck during a hunting accident. Mr. Johnson made two incisions to the cadaver's carotid artery and jugular vein. He then grabbed the man's arms and shook them up and down to increase circulation and blood evacuation. As blood surged from the cadaver's jugular vein, and flooded the embalming table, Mr. Johnson started injecting embalming fluid into the carotid artery. As I watched, I felt slightly terrified.

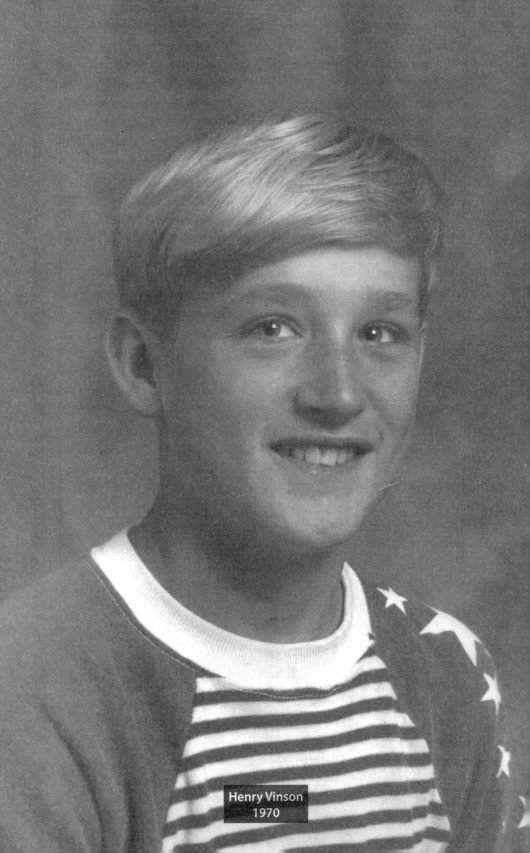

Henry Vinson
1970

CHAPTER FIVE

DREAMS

I graduated from high school with minimal fanfare—I didn't even attend the graduation ceremony. As a pre-graduation present, my mother bought me a red Toyota Celica that I drove back and forth from school in the latter half of my senior year, and I was ecstatic to see Williamson High School ebbing in its rearview mirror on my final day of high school. I had never managed to shake the overwhelming angst that seized me each morning when I awoke to attend one more day at Williamson High School—I felt like I was waking up in the middle of traffic every morning.

Within a couple of weeks after graduating from high school, I applied for an internship at the Ball Funeral Home, which was housed in a white, two-story Victorian-style house on the edge of downtown Williamson. The Ball Funeral Home was one of only three Williamson funeral homes that survived the flood of 1977, but its business had steadily declined since the flood.

I ultimately decided on the Ball Funeral Home for my internship, because M.T. Ball had become an idol of mine. I thought that he was the personification of compassion and the quintessence of a funeral director. Regrettably, by 1979, Mr. Ball had suffered a series of heart attacks and strokes that had left him incapacitated and nearly bedridden, so his wife, Justine, had assumed the day-to-day management of the funeral home.

On my initial visit to the Ball Funeral Home, I met with Mrs. Ball for an hour or so. She was in her mid-sixties, thin, and she wore a black Yves Saint Laurent dress. Mrs. Ball had the graceful and refined mannerisms of a patrician. Her maiden name was

Williamson, and the city of Williamson had been named after her forebears, so she considered herself to be Williamson aristocracy. Mrs. Ball was impeccably primped and preened. Her jet-black hair had hints of silver, and she had perfectly manicured and polished red nails. Although Mrs. Ball looked like she was on the threshold of stepping onto a Broadway stage, she had penetrating brown eyes and a stern demeanor. She had served a stint in the Army during World War II, and she projected an authoritative persona that reminded me of Uncle Clarence.

Mrs. Ball was a chain smoker, and her deep, raspy voice sounded like her larynx was made of sandpaper. She commenced the interview by inquiring if I was a homosexual. The Williamson grapevine had obviously preceded my interview. I think the grapevine of a small town has instantaneous communicative capabilities that nearly rival the Internet. My life's overriding ambition was to become a funeral director, and I needed to fulfill a funeral home internship before applying to mortuary schools, so I adamantly denied being gay. After I convinced Mrs. Ball that I wasn't a homosexual, she consented to my internship. My starting salary was $5.00 an hour.

In addition to an hourly wage, Mrs. Ball provided me with a furnished one-bedroom apartment that was on the second floor of the funeral home. The apartment was rather cozy, and its furbishing was a fusion of the garish interior decorating of the 1970s and a mausoleum. The thick, shag carpeting and walls were canary yellow, and its furnishings, bathroom fixtures, and kitchen appliances were black.

Since Mr. Ball had become debilitated, the funerals overseen by the Ball Funeral Home had dwindled, and Mrs. Ball was the funeral home's only full-time employee. Even the funeral director worked for Mrs. Ball on a part-time basis. So I quickly became a jack-of-all-trades. I answered phones at night, performed janitorial duties, assisted with the removal of cadavers and embalming, facilitated visitations, and I drove the flower car to funerals. I was overjoyed to play such an integral role at a funeral home, and I felt my life was progressing in a promising direction.

I also started to attend Southern West Virginia Community and Technical College. I planned on enrolling in a mortician school after I received my associate degree. Junior college was uneventful for me, but I actually began to enjoy school once more, because I could walk through the halls without being taunted.

I seemed to be in a state of perpetual motion as I toiled long hours at the funeral home and tackled full-time coursework at the junior college. As Mrs. Ball scrutinized my diligence and attentiveness, her frosty, rigid veneer started to thaw, and she became very much a maternal figure to me. The Balls lived across the street from the funeral home, and Mrs. Ball extended an open-ended invitation to me to have dinner with her family. Over the next two years, I rarely missed dinner with Mrs. Ball and her two daughters. Mr. Ball spent the majority of his day convalescing in bed. He was colorless, wizened, and frail, and I invariably felt a pang of pathos every time I caught a glimpse of him.

After I received an associate degree from Southern West Virginia Community and Technical College, I submitted an application to the Cincinnati College of Mortuary Science, because it was one of the premiere mortuary schools in the country. A month later, I received an acceptance letter.

Although my mother consented to underwrite my tuition and all of my expenses for mortuary school, she had emotionally distanced herself from me since I moved out of her house. I think a couple of factors played a role in her detachment. First, she had ceased being a bus driver and had become an entrepreneurial dynamo: She opened a second convenience store, and she also started an ambulance service and a retail cosmetics store. I think a second source of my mother's detachment was that she had started a new phase in her life, and she had consciously decided to wean me emotionally.

•••

In July 1981, my mother bought me a black Datsun 280Z. The following month, I packed it with nearly all of my worldly possessions and embarked for Cincinnati. By 1981, I had accumulated more than fifty cash registers, but I sensibly decided to leave them in my mother's basement. As I drove to Cincinnati, I felt tentative and, at the same time, eager. Cincinnati seemed like an immense, foreboding metropolis to me, but I was also extremely excited.

I moved into a house that was across the street from the Cincinnati College of Mortuary Science. The house had been haphazardly carved up into four furnished, studio apartments, and mine had beige walls and brown shag carpeting. The apartment barely accommodated a small kitchen and a loft bed. A small desk rested below the loft bed.

From the very first day, I thought mortuary school was fantastic, and I delighted in every facet of it. I found the classes—anatomy, physiology, restorative art, etc.—to be captivating, even exhilarating. One class, The History of Funeral Service, was particularly fascinating, and it was taught by Dr. Dan Flory, who would eventually become the Dean of the Cincinnati College of Mortuary Science. He was tall, fair-skinned, soft-spoken, and a very sharp dresser. A friendship that has endured to the present day gradually developed between us.

Shortly after my arrival in Cincinnati, I started riding my bicycle around Eden Park. The park has a maze of paved paths that wind around buildings and sculptures dating back to the early 1900s, and I found the sprawling, densely wooded park to be enchanting. I was inexplicably attracted to the park's large Moorish-style gazebo that was ornately painted in white and indigo and crowned by a spherical finial. A prominent Cincinnati attorney shot and murdered his wife at the gazebo in 1927, and legend has it that her ghost continues to haunt the gazebo.

Although I didn't encounter paranormal activity at the gazebo, I discovered that it was the epicenter of a burgeoning gay scene, but I was acutely shy and hesitant to entangle myself with anyone. After riding my bike to the gazebo every day for a couple of weeks, a tall, muscular man in his early thirties finally approached me. His name was Robert. He had thinning black hair and distinctive Mediterranean facial features—an aquiline nose, high cheekbones, and a dark complexion. Robert invited me to Friends, a gay bar near the park, and I agreed to accompany him.

When we entered Friends, I heard blaring disco music and a spinning mirrored ball scattered flashes of light throughout the bar. The bar was dark, and plumes of cigarette smoke wafted near the ceiling. As we crossed the black tiled floor and walked to a table near the bar, I was dumbfounded to see men kissing and holding hands. After Robert and I sat down, I ordered a coke, because I had never imbibed alcohol before. While I sipped my coke, and surveyed Friends' patrons, I quickly came to the visceral realization that I wasn't the only gay man in the world, and I was momentarily overwhelmed by jubilance. I finally had an existential affirmation of my sexuality.

Robert and I eventually wandered back to my apartment, and I had sex for the first time in my life. I had disclosed to Robert that I was a "virgin," so he was particularly caring and measured. His gentle glances, gestures, and caresses unlocked desires in me that had been an impermeable secret for years, and as he explored my body and I timidly explored his, those secrets ruptured into pyrotechnic bursts of bliss.

After we made love, Robert delicately embraced me. I was slightly surprised that the sheer joy enveloping me wouldn't be quelled by shame and apprehension. Robert and I dated for approximately three months. When I discovered that he was a priest, my perceptions of him were irrevocably altered, and we gradually drifted apart. Nevertheless, I continued to patronize Friends on an almost nightly basis. I initially felt socially awkward in the confines of a bar, so I tended to play Pac-Man by myself. But I eventually befriended a couple of guys who were about my age, and they introduced me to Badlands, Cincinnati's largest gay bar. Badlands was in the warehouse district of Cincinnati, and it was vast. Whereas Friends accommodated maybe 100 patrons a night, Badlands was an undulating sea of 500 men. Over the course of my two years in Cincinnati, I dated ten men whom I met at Badlands.

As I negotiated my nascent sexuality, I navigated my first semester of mortuary school with great ease, because I found the curriculum so interesting and stimulating. Although I was indeed in the midst of actualizing my dream of becoming a funeral director, I also dreamed of becoming a pilot. After I checked out flight schools around the Cincinnati area, I phoned my mother and broached the subject with her. She was initially hesitant, but I assured her that flight school wouldn't interfere with my studies, so she reluctantly consented to fund my pursuit of a pilot's license.

I enrolled in Cardinal Air Training flight school, and my first solo was in a Cessna 150 on January 19th, 1982. As I soloed, I experienced the same sense of liberation I felt as an 11-year-old soaring out of the Huntington Tri-State Airport to visit Uncle Clarence, and flying continues to be one of the greatest joys of my life. In addition to being a major benchmark en route to my pilot's license, my first solo flight was a momentous occasion as my brother had been slated to solo just before his death.

Despite attending mortuary school and flight school full time, I managed to hit either Friends or Badlands just about every night. I loved attending both schools, and I also loved awakening my libido from its prolonged hibernation. I was only twenty-one at the time, so I had the vitality and boundless energy of youth. I felt like I had transcended the vestiges of my hellish teenage years, and I was floating in paradise.

I received my pilot's license in May 1982, and four months later I graduated from the Cincinnati College of Mortuary Science. I think a rational course of action would've been to canvas major metropolitan areas, where gays weren't considered pariahs, in my quest to be a funeral director. Since I was a child, however, I envisioned myself as a funeral director in Williamson, West Virginia, and my driving ambition imparted blinders that prevented me from seeing that returning to Williamson wouldn't be optimal. But I ultimately made the irrational decision of venturing back to the future.

•••

Upon my return to Williamson, I assumed the mantle of funeral director for the Ball Funeral Home, and I again found myself residing in the funeral home's second-story apartment. I felt that my newfound upward mobility necessitated a new wardrobe, so after a week or so I strolled into the Man Shop Limited in Williamson, and I bought myself a handful of Brooks Brothers suits.

I had been the funeral director of Ball Funeral Home for three months when I discovered that Mingo County was in need of a medical examiner. At the time, Mingo County was a cauldron of corruption, and Johnnie Owens was its Democratic political boss. He was the county's de facto behind-the-scenes mover and shaker. My mother and Johnnie Owens were old friends, dating back to grammar school, and I mentioned to her that I had an interest in becoming the Mingo County medical examiner. A few days after our conversation, I received a phone call from Johnnie Owens, and then I met with him at his office in the Mingo County Courthouse in Williamson.

Johnnie Owens was short and stocky. As he sat behind an enormous oak desk, he emanated an imposing persona, even though he was casually dressed in black slacks and a white button-down shirt. Although he spoke in a tranquil drawl, he had piercing obsidian eyes. Owens wasn't a man who parsed words, and he quickly inquired if I would like to be Mingo County Medical Examiner. After I reconfirmed my ambition to him, our meeting concluded.

A couple of weeks later, the chief medical examiner of West Virginia phoned me, and I quickly found myself the new Mingo County medical examiner. I was offered an office at the courthouse in Williamson, but I declined the offer, because I felt that my office at the Ball Funeral Home could also facilitate my responsibilities as the county's medical examiner. Shortly after my appointment, I bought a 1977 Cessna 172.

My father had constantly demeaned me as "worthless," and the abuse and cruelty I had suffered at Williamson High School only served to reinforce my father's degradations. By the age of twenty-two years old, however, I had actualized my life's wildest dreams by becoming a funeral director, medical examiner, and a pilot, but my wildest dreams had a secret caveat: I had to live a lie. I embraced the illusion that wedding my work would nullify my sexuality, but I occasionally flew my Cessna to Cincinnati, rented a hotel room, and visited Badlands and Friends.

As the Mingo County Medical Examiner, I had a beeper, and I was on call twenty-four hours a day, 364 days a year. I often had to venture to the most remote corners of Mingo County, in the middle of the night, to make official pronouncements of death. If I determined that a death was due to natural causes, I would issue an immediate a death certificate. But if I determined that the death was accidental, I would order toxicology testing before issuing a death certificate. In the rare event of a suicide, perceived foul play, or a death that occurred in a correctional institution, it was mandatory that I order an autopsy.

Mingo County was sparsely populated, and I tended to approximately 80 deaths a year. The county compensated me on a per case basis, and I continued to be the full-time funeral director at the Ball Funeral Home. Despite an income of around $60,000 a year between the two jobs, I still lived in the apartment on the second floor of the Ball Funeral Home. I didn't have to pay rent or utilities, and I had dinner with the Balls on most nights. The Balls felt like family to me.

CHAPTER SIX

D.C.

As I managed the Ball Funeral Home and met my responsibilities as Mingo County Medical Examiner, my mother underwent an unforeseen metamorphosis. She developed an undying friendship with an affluent widow named Ethel Polis. Mrs. Polis was extremely religious, and she shepherded my mother back into the fold. My mother's newfound religious conversion had a major affect on my life. First and foremost, she began to have reservations about my sexuality, which I found rather disconcerting. Secondly, Mrs. Polis and my mother decided to travel the world and spread the "word." Their first stop was Haiti.

Although my mother thought I was immersed in the wages of sin, she presented me with the deeds to her house and a handful of buildings she owned in Nolan before she embarked for Haiti. My mother also handed me sole proprietorship of a convenience store. My estranged father, Charles Vinson, had since "retired" to a life of ubiquitous vodka consumption, and he became extremely homicidal, because he didn't receive a cut from the spoils of my mother's religious rebirth. He dispatched death threats to me via the phone, and he even barged into the convenience store brandishing a pistol. After I secured a restraining order against him, he sued me. Given my father's homicidal bent, I felt it was prudent to quickly settle his lawsuit. I sold the properties in Nolan, and I gave him the proceeds from one of the buildings.

By 1985, Mrs. Ball had started to appear elderly and frail, so I floated her a generous offer to purchase the Ball Funeral Home. I thought she would welcome my offer with open arms, because it would afford her a comfortable retirement, but she became bellicose and downright nasty. Rage distorted the prim contours of her face as she snapped that she would never sell the Ball Funeral Home to me.

After that exchange, our relationship disintegrated, and I decided to make my entrepreneurial leap: I resigned from the Ball Funeral Home and opened the Vinson Funeral Home. The Allen Funeral Home in downtown Williamson had been vacant since the flood of 1977, so I signed one-year lease for the building. I had it refurbished and brought up to code, and I purchased a hearse. I continued to be the Mingo County Medical Examiner.

Much to my chagrin, Mrs. Ball equated my entrepreneurial leap with matricide. She vowed that I would suffer severe consequences, and I seriously underestimated her wrath. Mrs. Ball quickly recruited funeral home owners in the Williamson area, and they jumped on her bandwagon due to economic self-interest: They were already contending with a dearth of funerals and a new funeral home would only exacerbate their plight. I think that the funeral homes around Williamson realized that the upstart Vinson Funeral Home would be a threat to their livelihoods when Williamson's police chief died, and his family arranged his funeral through my funeral home.

The funeral home directors formed a vicious circle, and they conscripted a prominent Williamson attorney to write a letter to the West Virginia medical examiner that accused me of using my position as Mingo County medical examiner to solicit business, which was absolutely false. Whenever I visited the scene of a death, I would hand out my medical examiner's card to the family of the deceased—I never handed them my personal business cards.

As the smear campaign against me intensified, M.T. Ball, Jr., returned to Williamson. He had been charged with falsifying a prescription in an adjacent county, and he decided to lay low at his mother's house. M.T. Ball, Jr., had been the Balls' prodigal son, and he occasionally visited his family while I worked at their funeral home. Shortly after M.T. Ball, Jr., arrived in Williamson, one of his friends barged into my funeral home—he said his car had broken down and requested to use my phone. I thought his behavior was rather odd as he repeatedly dialed a number and then abruptly hung up the phone. Unbeknownst to me, he had repeatedly phoned the Ball Funeral Home.

I should say it was unbeknownst to me until I was charged with making harassing phone calls to the Ball Funeral Home. Although the charge was a misdemeanor, I was innocent and decided to fight it. But the magistrate overseeing the case was a friend of Mrs. Ball's, and he promptly found me guilty. I appealed his decision, and I ultimately agreed to a plea bargain: I would resign as Mingo County medical examiner and the misdemeanor charge would be dropped.

As Ball et al. were besieging me, a dour widow named Mrs. Marcum visited me. She was a short, bony woman in her early fifties, who had the ravages of Appalachia hardship carved on her face. Mrs. Marcum's husband had been a coal miner who died of natural causes. Since her husband's death, Mrs. Marcum had been quickly reduced to welfare. The state of West Virginia subsidized the funerals of welfare recipients to the tune of $650, even though the average cost of an interment was around $3,000, so funeral homes in the Williamson area had declined to perform Mr. Marcum's funeral.

I felt sorry for Mrs. Marcum, and I consented to carry out her husband's funeral. Although the state specified that the deceased of welfare recipients were to be interred in wooden, cloth-covered caskets, I buried Mr. Marcum in a metal casket. I had performed three state subsidized funerals prior to Mr. Marcum, and I used metal caskets for those funerals too, because I thought that wooden, cloth-covered caskets looked dreadful and highlighted the deceased's indigence. I believed that an individual should be buried with a baseline of respect and decency. Despite upgrading the caskets for state subsidized funerals, I billed the state its standard $650. Mr. Marcum's body was interred at Mountain View Memory Gardens, where Butch had been buried. I carried out Mr. Marcum's funeral flawlessly, but its aftermath would mark the beginning of the end for me Williamson.

•••

A couple of weeks after Mr. Marcum's burial, I received a call from the manager of Mountain View Memory Gardens. He sounded exasperated as he told me that Mrs. Marcum had phoned the cemetery several times a day, demanding that her husband's body be exhumed. Mountain View Memory Gardens had finally acquiesced and requested that I pick up the body. I collected the remains of Mr. Marcum later that day.

After her husband's funeral, Mrs. Marcum had been notified about the Black Lung Benefits Act, which is a federal program that provides monthly benefits to coal miners with black lung disease or their surviving dependents, and she required an autopsy to determine if her husband had died of black lung disease. I explained to Mrs. Marcum that the state wasn't authorized to perform an autopsy on a death due to natural causes, so the autopsy had to be performed by a pathologist in private practice. I eventually found a pathologist in Beckley, West Virginia, which is more than 100 miles from Williamson, to perform the autopsy. I then informed Mrs. Marcum that the pathologist's fee would be approximately $2,000, but she dawdled. After three or four weeks, I broached the subject with Mrs. Marcum once more, and she refused to shell out a nickel.

Mrs. Marcum eventually approached Mrs. Ball or vice-versa, and, needless to say, the former provided the latter and her clique with the fodder to taint the upstart Vinson Funeral Home. The newspaper reported that I kept Mr. Marcum's body at my funeral home for "42 days," because of Mrs. Marcum's inability to pay me. Unfortunately, the newspaper neglected to mention that I had previously buried Mr. Marcum, and also the exact circumstances for Mr. Marcum's prolonged respite at my funeral home. After I funded Mr. Marcum's autopsy out of my own pocket, I thought that would be the end my difficulties, but I was woefully wrong.

In the wake of being charged with making harassing phone calls, I was then charged with a second misdemeanor—obtaining state monies under false pretenses. The statutes specifying that wooden, cloth-covered caskets be used for state subsidized funerals were extremely stringent, so upgrading the four welfare recipients, including Mr. Marcum, to metal caskets was technically illegal, even though I didn't charge the state beyond its standard $650 fee. After I repatriated my charges for the four funerals to the state—$2,600—that misdemeanor charge was dropped too. But the latter onslaught essentially doomed the Vinson Funeral Home.

Throughout my brief tenure as the proprietor of the Vinson Funeral Home, the *Williamson Daily News* was invariably derisive when it reported on my travails. The newspaper's articles made me out to be the Beelzebub of funeral directors. I think the *Williamson Daily News'* skewed coverage of me was primarily due to its lead reporter on the Henry Vinson beat being the sister-in-law of one of Williamson's funeral home owners. Although bad press saturated me, and I had to contend with the ire of Williamson's judiciary, I was never disciplined by the West Virginia Board of Funeral Service Examiners, because, at least, it realized that I hadn't committed any improprieties.

I realize that I'm a two-time convicted felon—albeit my second conviction was a government frame as I will explain—and I also realize that some of the circumstances precipitating my demise as the Mingo County medical examiner and, for that matter, a mortician in West Virginia ultimately boil down to a he-said, she-said quandary. But I think there's one incontrovertible indication that a mendacious smear campaign was waged again me: Mrs. Marcum's daughter declared that I was the illegitimate father of her child!

I subsequently decided to follow my mortuary fortunes to Washington, D.C. Despite the fact that my life's ambition was to be merely a funeral director in Williamson, West Virginia, I regrettably discovered that being the focal point of petulant morticians dedicated to preserving their market share and of a hostile small town newspaper was just a dress rehearsal for my sojourn to Washington, D.C., where I became the focal point of malevolent feds dedicated to preserving their secrets and of a duplicitous *Washington Post*. Indeed, I would find that the Justice Department, Secret Service, and the country's media elites are infinitely more malicious than the bullies at Williamson High School or the morticians of Williamson. So Washington, D.C. was, unfortunately, upward mobility—Henry Vinson style.

•••

When I embarked for D.C., I left the vast majority of my possessions at my mother's house, but my 280Z was laden with clothes. The drive was about eight hours, and I spent the first four hours smothered by a thick pathos as I contended with a relentless cascade of tears. I had naively assumed that I would be in Williamson for the duration of my life, and I felt a strong bond to the various families I had served as a funeral director. I thought I was abandoning them. However, I had grudgingly embraced the fact that I had to leave Williamson if I were to have a future as a funeral director.

Given the vagaries of my life, I've never automatically defaulted to the idea that the future is friendly. But as I drove through Virginia on Highway 81, my pathos gradually started to fragment—albeit bit-by-bit. I started to feel a tenuous sense of liberation as I came to the realization that D.C. had the potential to be a fresh start for me. Throughout my years in Williamson, I had to don a guise of lies everyday to conceal my sexuality, and it had become increasingly cumbersome and untenable. I decided to discard the lies about my sexuality in my D.C. incarnation, and as the capital drew nearer and nearer I started to feel a sense of exhilaration that had been absent from my life since Cincinnati. I also sincerely thought that I could bid adieu to the events that had precipitated my demise in Williamson. I didn't realize that those events were a specter slumbering in the shadows that would awaken nearly four years later to haunt me.

I had been to the D.C. area on numerous occasions, because my mother's favorite sister, Josephine, lived in Silver Spring, Maryland. Aunt Josephine had divorced years earlier. Her former husband owned a construction company that specialized in high-rise commercial buildings, and their divorce left her comfortably situated. Aunt Josephine had four children, but her oldest son, Gus, died in a freak construction accident when he was seventeen years old. So Aunt Josephine and my mother shared a bond that had been forged from the deaths of their oldest sons. When we visited Aunt Josephine, she and my mother spent hours commiserating over the losses of their sons. Like Aunt Josephine, my mother never transcended the death of her son. Until the day she died, she had "BUTCH" inscribed on her personalized license plates.

Silver Spring is a suburban, bedroom community of D.C., and Josephine lived in a split-level brick house on a street that was lined with oak trees. Before departing Williamson, I phoned and told her my plans to relocate to the D.C. area. Her three children were in their early thirties, so she had an empty nest, and she generously offered to accommodate me.

After I rang the doorbell, Aunt Josephine greeted me with a hospitable hug. She was in her mid-fifties, lithe, and stunningly attractive. She had shoulder length brunette hair and loving bronze eyes. She had been gifted with all of the beauty genes that had rippled through my maternal grand parents' gene pool.

Aunt Josephine directed me to an upstairs bedroom, where I deposited my clothes. Then we sat in her living room, talking about our family, my mother, and my plans. Aunt Josephine, like my mother, was extremely religious, but she was more cheerful and upbeat than my mother. Although I felt grateful for Aunt Josephine's hospitality, I didn't want impose on her, so I immediately started looking for employment and a flat.

I contacted a fellow mortician named Jeff who had also grown up in Williamson. Jeff was ten years older than me, and our paths hadn't crossed until we met at a funeral directors tradeshow a few years earlier. When we met, Jeff was working as a funeral director in Charleston, West Virginia, and I found him to be quite gracious.

Although Jeff was gay, he had been living a secret life with a wife and two children. Jeff's penchant to preserve his secret life had gradually eroded, so he divorced and moved to the D.C. area. Jeff and I shared the mutual inferno of growing up gay in rural West Virginia, and also a passion for death care. Our common denominators translated into an instant friendship.

I had been at Josephine's for few days when I rendezvoused with Jeff for dinner at a Bob's Big Boy in Lanham, Maryland. He lived about ten miles from Aunt Josephine in Lanham. Jeff was pudgy and medium height. He had thinning dark hair and dark eyes, and his round, ruddy face had extensive acne scarring. He had an extremely extroverted, alpha male personality.

As we had dinner, Jeff suggested that I contact the Chambers Funeral Homes, which were headquartered in Riverdale, Maryland. He had briefly served as a funeral director there, and he said that Chambers was in need of a funeral director. Jeff also had a one-bedroom apartment, and he offered his couch to me. So within a week of arriving at Aunt Josephine's house, I moved into Jeff's apartment.

The day after I met Jeff at Bob's Big Boy, I phoned the Chambers Funeral Homes and arranged an interview for the following day. The Chambers Funeral Homes had three branches around the D.C. area, and I interviewed at their Riverdale headquarters. The Riverdale branch was housed in white, three-story colonial mansion with a mansard roof. As I entered the funeral home, I stepped onto a plush red carpet, and an elderly woman with shoulder-length gray hair in a lavender dress, sitting at the reception desk, gave me a genuine, heartfelt smile as if I were a prospective bereaved patron.

I introduced myself, and she motioned to a chair that was next to her desk. After I sat down, she ambled up the stairway, and I panned the funeral home's pristine, opulent interior. The funeral home had a lavish interior that was unlike the funeral homes in Williamson. Accordingly, the Chambers Funeral Homes were vastly different than the funeral homes of Williamson in terms of volume: Williamson had maybe 100 funerals a year, and the Chambers Funeral Homes supervised four or five funerals a day.

Shortly after I sat down, William Chambers III skirted down the stairs. He was tall, corpulent, and balding. William III, whose nickname was Billy, greeted me with enthusiastic brown eyes and a smile that was brimming with white teeth. He wore a brown three-piece suit. After he thrust out his thick, silky soft right hand and introduced himself, I followed him up the stairs, where he ushered me into his second floor office. Given the funeral home's posh interior, I was surprised that his suit was relatively inexpensive.

Billy interviewed me for an hour or so. He didn't have the refinement and polish of many of the funeral directors I had previously encountered, but he was very down-to-earth, and he had a great sense of humor. In fact, he is one of the nicest guys I've ever met. Billy hired me on the spot, and a few days later I was a funeral director at the Chambers Funeral Homes. Billy managed the funeral homes with his two younger brothers—Tommy and Robert. Robert managed the Silver Spring, Maryland branch.

The Chambers Funeral Homes had a fabled history in the D.C. area. The three Chambers brothers were fourth generation morticians. Their grandfather, William W. Chambers, Sr., was extremely flamboyant, and he founded W.W. Chambers Company in the 1920s. W.W., Sr., had a panache for advertising. One of his promotional campaigns included an advertising calendar featuring the reproduction of a nude young woman that stated "Beautiful Bodies by Chambers." He also proffered a motto that W.W. Chambers Company was "The largest undertaker in the world." The Federal Trade Commission took exception to his boast, so in 1937 he amended his motto to "One of the largest undertakers in the world." At the time of my employment, a towering red fluorescent sign atop the Riverdale branch snapped "One of the largest undertakers in the world" into the night.

The Chambers' grandfather bequeathed the business to his son—W.W., Jr., who spent six months out of every year in D.C. and six months in Pompano, Florida. W.W., Jr., was fond of yachting, and he lived a leisurely life. He was short with slicked back gray hair. When he was in D.C., he drove his blue Cadillac around to the family's three funeral homes and flower shop every day. Dressed in impeccable suits, he floated in and out of the funeral homes. His sons and the funeral homes' employees treated him as a visiting dignitary, and Billy essentially ran the business' day-to-day operations.

I initially found the funeral home to be daunting due to its sheer volume. The Chambers Funeral Homes oversaw around 1,500 funerals a year. My initial tasks were transporting cadavers to the funeral home and embalming. The latter is my least favorite facet of being a mortician. I find formaldehyde extremely malodorous, and the scent of an autopsied cadaver isn't very pleasant either.

Billy quickly realized that my strong suit as a mortician was counseling grieving families, and I eventually started to work with families. I was sincerely devoted to comforting mourning families. I'm fond of helping families set up their ideal service, and then implementing it perfectly. I generally worked from 8:00 A.M. to 5:00 P.M. seven days a week, because I loved being a funeral director and my social life was fairly nonexistent.

I wasn't familiar with the D.C. area, so Billy would draw me meticulous and intricate maps when I led funeral processions with the hearse. I had been employed by the Chambers Funeral Home about a month when I was tasked with leading a funeral procession down the beltway to a cemetery in Quantico, Virginia. The procession consisted of approximately forty cars, and I veered onto the wrong exit. I pulled over on the exit ramp, and explained my miscue to the startled family. The entire procession then followed me as I circled back to the correct exit. It's always been extremely important for me to implement flawless funerals, so I found that tremendously embarrassing.

A second unforgettable mortuary moment occurred on Christmas day 1986. I was embalming an emaciated elderly man who had been autopsied. The medical personnel who performed the autopsy had left a needle in the cadaver's superior vena cava. The needle sliced my forearm, and, as I pulled my forearm from the cadaver, the cut brushed against the cadaver's ribcage. In 1986, hospitals generally didn't provide cause of death documentation that accompanied a cadaver to the funeral home since HIV was extremely rare.

Within a week of performing the autopsy, I received the man's death certificate, and I glanced over it as I sat at my office desk. The death certificate stated that the man had hepatitis A and B, and he died of AIDS. I was devastated. I immediately contacted a physician, and a blood test confirmed that I contracted hepatitis A and B, but fortunately I evaded HIV. Although I felt extremely ill for several weeks, I managed to drag myself to work every day.

I crashed on Jeff's couch for the next six months as I acclimated to D.C. I eventually found a one-bedroom, basement apartment on the 1700 block of New Hampshire Avenue Northwest in a postwar, seven-story brick building, which was five blocks from DuPont Circle. The apartment had beige walls and a newly lacquered hardwood floor. I didn't have the inclination to retrieve my furniture from Williamson, so I opted for a shopping spree at Ethan Allen.

Once I had my new apartment comfortably furnished, and it started to feel like home, I visited West Virginia and retrieved my Cessna. I stored it at the Montgomery County Airport in Maryland. Around that time, I started visiting D.C.'s National Air and Space Museum every Saturday morning. The National Air and Space Museum has the largest collection of historic aircraft and spacecraft in the world, and I found it enthralling. It also had an IMAX theater that I thought was amazing: I found myself watching *Threshold: The Blue Angels Experience* every Saturday for weeks on end. Although I wandered through the museum nearly every Saturday throughout my tenure in D.C., I never tired of the exhibits, and I liked to have lunch in the museum's cafeteria.

The D.C. gay scene was a major departure from my prior experience. The gay bars had hundreds and hundreds of patrons, and walking through DuPont Circle, I glimpsed gay couples holding hands in public. I dined in restaurants whose patrons were primarily gay. I also noticed that many gay men appeared to have successful careers. I finally felt like I had the right to be gay. I eschewed all pretenses of being straight. I accepted my sexuality on a level that was unparalleled to the acceptance I had realized when I was in Cincinnati.

Following my move, Jeff and I continued pal around D.C. Although Jeff had a placid exterior, he was a wild man, who loved to drink and hit the bars. I was considerably more conservative, and I've never cultivated a taste for booze. It's very difficult for me to imbibe the first drink. After the first drink has made my palate less discriminating, I have less difficulty with the second drink, but three drinks is generally my limit. When Jeff and I would hit a bar, I nursed a drink or two as I watched him pound down ten to twelve drinks in staccato succession. Jeff quickly introduced me Shooters, an exotic dance bar, on the corner of Massachusetts and 20th Street Northwest, near DuPont Circle. Shooters was on the third floor of the Rigs Bank building, and as Jeff and I climbed the stairs to Shooters, I had no idea that I was about to be transported to an alternative universe. When Jeff opened the door, I instantly collided with a tsunami of blaring music. We seated ourselves at a mahogany bar with brass fixtures that extended for about 30 feet.

Shooters was wedged in a narrow room, and the mahogany bar nearly stretched the distance of the room. Shooters had black walls, and it was dimly lit—except for the spotlights illuminating the six Adonis-like men who danced and gyrated atop the bar. The dancers were perfect manifestations of the male physique, and they were scantily clad in jock straps and tube socks. The men sitting at the bar and milling around tucked bills into their tube socks as they danced. Shooters was like a Dionysian dreamscape to me.

I never mustered the courage to visit Shooters by myself, because I was still painfully shy and awkward in the context of social milieus, but Jeff and I hit Shooters two or three times a week. Crossing the threshold of Shooters was the first event in a chain of events that transformed me from a mild mannered mortician into a D.C. madam. Shooters was essentially the neutron fired into plutonium that initiated a nuclear reaction, and unfortunately my life would be its Ground Zero.

Chambers Funeral Home

CHAPTER SEVEN

NIGHTLIFE

As I periodically explored D.C.'s gay scene by night, I woke up every morning at 6:00 A.M. I started work at the funeral home at 8:00 A.M., so I had a leisurely cushion of two hours to prepare myself to meet the day. On most mornings I bumped into Robert Chambers, who was the youngest of the Chambers brothers. Although he managed the branch in Silver Spring, Maryland, he lived next to the Riverdale branch, and he briefly popped into the Riverdale branch in the mornings for mail and various miscellanies. After Robert collected his mail, and chatted with Billy for a few minutes, he would hop into his blue Mazda RX7 and drive to Silver Spring.

Robert was a youthful looking 35 years old. He had bleached blond hair and brown eyes, but he wore blue contact lenses. He was medium height and very slender. Robert had a fashion sense that was markedly different than his brothers. The first time I was introduced to Robert he wore a black Brooks Brother's suit, a pink shirt, and a pink tie. Robert lived with his wife and three children, but his mannerisms were extremely effeminate, and his brother Tommy incessantly teased him about being gay.

Robert had a quick wit, and our morning interactions initially consisted of cursory greetings and superficial, witty banter as he darted in and out of the Riverdale branch. But after a couple of months, Robert and I started having protracted conversations. One night, after work, Robert and I made a trek to Shooters. Robert was quite familiar with Shooters, and he struck me as terribly discontented due to his secret life.

I had been at the Riverdale branch for about six months when Robert requested that I transfer to the Silver Spring branch. The

Silver Spring branch arranged around fifteen funerals a week, and Robert was the branch's only funeral director. Robert felt overwhelmed, and my forte as a mortician was working with mourning families, so my reassignment to Silver Spring was a sound move.

The Silver Spring branch was housed in a three-story brick building located near the bustling intersection of Georgia Avenue and Fenton Street. The ground floor had a regal marble foyer and thirty-foot ceilings. An office was to the left of the entrance, and a picturesque chapel was situated behind a wall of frosted glass. The basement accommodated Robert's office and my office and arrangement rooms, where Robert and I discussed funeral arrangements with clients. The basement also featured a large show room that consisted of thirty different caskets that clients could consider purchasing.

During my first six months at Silver Spring, Robert and I regularly hit Shooters, and Jeff would often accompany us. I gradually found myself becoming infatuated with one of Shooters' dancers. He was around 5'8", breathtakingly handsome, and he had a magnificent physique. Though all of the dancers at Shooters were breathtakingly handsome with magnificent physiques, this particular dancer had shoulder length black hair, a smooth, dark complexion, and blue eyes that sparkled like sapphires floating in white enamel. His eyes were mesmerizing.

I was far too shy to initiate a conversation with the dancer, but Jeff sensed that I had taken a fancy to him. After Jeff stuffed a handful of bills into his tube socks, he invited the dancer to sit with us. Jeff introduced himself to the dancer, and then he introduced me. The dancer's name was Jimmy, and his tube socks were bulging and overflowing with bills. Jeff cajoled me into inviting Jimmy on a dinner date—and Jimmy accepted.

•••

The following night, I met Jimmy at a restaurant named Two Quail. Jimmy was a few minutes late, and he wore a white T-shirt, beige shorts, and tennis shoes. Two Quail was in an old row house about three blocks from Capitol Hill, and it had a garish, chic interior. The tables and chairs scattered throughout the cozy restaurant didn't match. In fact, the silverware and plates didn't match either. Our tall, tattooed and pierced waiter was the human embodiment of Two Quail's garish chic. I ordered stuffed chicken breast, and Jimmy also ordered stuffed chicken breast. After dinner, as we sipped on red wine, Jimmy divulged that he was an escort as well as a dancer. I had never met an escort before, and I was stunned. Jimmy then piped that he made between $1,000 and $2,000 a day as an escort.

I'm fascinated by business, and I was particularly captivated by Jimmy's disclosures, so I plied him with questions. He was quite candid as he discussed the various nuances of the escort business. Jimmy then informed me that an escort service that employed him, Ebony and Ivory, was for sale. When I inquired about the figure, I initially thought the price would be astronomical, but, surprisingly, Jimmy replied the owner sought a mere $10,000. I surmised that if Jimmy made $1,000 a day, I could probably make my investment back in a couple of weeks. Jimmy intuited that my internal ten-key adding machine was crunching numbers, and he proposed that I meet the owner of Ebony and Ivory. I replied that I had to give it a little thought.

As I drove home that night, I ruminated about purchasing Ebony and Ivory, which was certainly out of character for me. I was puzzled by Jimmy's description of Ebony and Ivory's owner and his operation of the business, because it seemed that the escort service was run in an inept, slipshod manner. According to Jimmy, the owner was lackadaisical about answering the phones, and only fielded calls when he felt like it.

When I returned to my apartment, I flipped through the D.C. Yellow Pages and found Ebony and Ivory under male escort services. The fact that the business was advertised in the Yellow Pages gave it legitimacy in my eyes. A few days later, I phoned Jimmy, and he consented to set up a meeting between the owner of Ebony and Ivory and me.

Jimmy lived in a townhouse on Maryland Avenue, where he rented a room. After I rang the doorbell, Jimmy greeted me in his customary white T-shirt and beige shorts. His bedroom was overflowing with plastic elephants, porcelain elephants, bronze elephants, ceramic elephants, etc. The artwork on the walls depicted elephants, and he collected books on elephants. Jimmy's grand plan was to open a boutique that catered exclusively to elephant aficionados. In retrospect, I should've realized that Jimmy had an affinity for drugs, but my prior interactions with druggies were practically nonexistent, so I thought his grand plan was the byproduct of eccentricity instead of synthetic opiates. I was in the midst of a sharp learning curve.

After I collected Jimmy, we rendezvoused with the owner of Ebony and Ivory, Richard, at his condominium in the Car Barn on Capitol Hill. The Car Barn was a sprawling brick building that been used to store D.C. buses in the 1960s, but in the 1970s a private developer converted the building into condominiums. I parked on 14th Street Southeast, and I felt extremely anxious as Jimmy and I walked to the Car Barn.

Richard greeted us at the door of his condominium. He was maybe 5'5", and he had thick black hair and sunken, brown eyes. He was clad in a white robe and wearing slippers. His skin was sallow, and he was emaciated. He looked like a skeleton that was enveloped by a thin veil of clay as he slowly crept into the living room. As we sat in Richard's living room, I discretely panned Richard's two-story dwelling, which had beige walls and hardwood floors. His condominium was furbished with contemporary furnishings, and its walls were tastefully garnished with post-modernist art.

Richard was barely treading over death's abyss, and he was forthright about the fact that he was dying from AIDS. He slowly enunciated his words, and his mannerisms were labored. Richard had become too physically incapacitated to contend with the operation of his escort service, so he wanted to extricate himself from it. I inquired about advertising, and he replied that he advertised in various venues, but he was uncertain about which were cost effective. After our hour-long meeting, I concluded that Ebony and Ivory had the potential to be a lucrative business if it were competently managed. But I balked at making a definitive decision, and I told Richard that I would give him a yea or nay within the week.

When the meeting with Richard concluded, Jimmy and I met a friend of Jimmy's for dinner. Jimmy's friend, Chris, was an extremely handsome man in his mid-twenties. He was tall and slender with flaxen, blond hair and blue eyes—he looked like a Swedish model. Chris was an escort too, and, over dinner, he and Jimmy ranted about the various glitches and difficulties they encountered working for escort services. I was still tangled up in ambivalence about whether or not I should purchase Ebony and Ivory until Chris revealed that on rare occasions he made upwards of $10,000 a day as an escort. Chris' disclosure was the critical mass I needed to purchase Ebony and Ivory. I wrote Richard a check the next day.

After I bought Ebony and Ivory, I started to receive ten to fifteen calls a day for escorts, and I became very, very busy. Initially, I had a beeper, and I personally fielded all the calls placed to Ebony and Ivory. After I talked to a prospective patron, I phoned Jimmy, who handled the arrangements for an escort to be sent to the patron's location. As it turned out, all of Jimmy's friends were escorts, so I had an instant pool of employees. Our average session was $150: The escort received 60 percent, I received 40 percent, and I compensated Jimmy with a weekly salary.

The business didn't seem overly outlandish to me, because I was accustomed to being on call 24 hours a day. Plus, I exclusively dealt with consenting adults, so I didn't have ethical quandaries about running an escort service. My primary ethical concern was the safety of the escorts, and I gave them strict instructions to phone me before and after their appointments.

In mortuary school, I found the marketing classes particularly interesting, and I pondered various strategies to nurture my business. One night I found myself paging through the D.C. Yellow Pages and phoning escort services. Escort services are often fly-by-night ventures, and their owners often abscond without paying their phone bills. So as I phoned the escort services in the D.C. Yellow Pages, I noticed many of the numbers had been disconnected.

73

The following day, I phoned the telephone company and offered to remunerate it for the arrears on the disconnected phone numbers in the Yellow Pages in exchange for ownership of the numbers. I quickly acquired around twenty additional phone numbers, and my business started to boom.

I've always been fascinated by cash registers, office equipment, and phone systems, and I had a Merlin phone system installed in my apartment, which gave me an additional forty telephone lines, enabling me to assimilate the phone numbers I had acquired from trolling the Yellow Pages.

After I installed the Merlin phone system, Jimmy arranged escort appointments from my apartment throughout the day, and I arranged escort appointments throughout the night. I loved being a funeral director, so I never even considered quitting the Chambers Funeral Homes. Indeed, Robert and I were the business' frontrunners in funeral sales. At the sprite age of twenty-six years old, I was a funeral director by day and a D.C. madam by night.

The Yellow Pages' ads significantly enlarged my business. So I renewed the various ads in the Yellow pages the following year, and I purchased additional ads under five categories: escorts, entertainment, companion, gay advocacy, and travel companion. I also advertised in the *Washington Blade* and D.C.'s weekly *City Paper*.

By the end of 1987, I started to reap more than 100 calls daily. The sheer volume of calls made my Merlin phone system obsolete, and I acquired a T1 phone line, which offered me a bank of 100 phone numbers that I had the capability of activating or deactivating. The T1 essentially gave me a mini phone company in the humble confines of my living room. After I acquired the T1, I placed scores of personal ads in the *City Paper* on a weekly basis that were accompanied by different phone numbers. The T1 allowed me to see the various phone lines that lit up, and answer the phone according to the respective ad that elicited the phone call. I also competed with myself due to the various ads I had placed in the Yellow Pages, so the T1 allowed me to distinguish those various phone numbers too.

I had up to 20 escorts working on a given night, and I ultimately installed a chalkboard in my living room. A quick glance at the chalkboard enabled me to identify the escorts working on a given night, and if they were out on calls. The chalkboard enabled me to track the escorts' whereabouts too, because their safety was a paramount concern for me. I also bought a Macintosh II, and I had a program written that identified patrons by their phone numbers. So when they phoned, I would type their respective phone numbers into the computer, and it would instantly reveal their preferred escorts or their respective preferences.

As the volume of calls for escorts started to escalate, I found the beeper to be inadequate, and I eventually had a phone installed in one of the funeral home's showroom caskets. The phone rested under the casket's lower lid, so it was concealed from the funeral home's employees and clientele. Only Robert and I were privy to the casket hotline. I found that one phone could suffice during the day, because the vast majority of my calls came at night. The T1 typically didn't start lighting up until 8:00 P.M.

I have to confess that I found my escort business to be intoxicating. People of unsurpassed beauty surrounded me, and they made me feel like the most important person in their life since I was integral to their livelihood. My sexuality had been a nightmare for me in my earlier years, and now, finally, I had scores of people affirming my sexuality. It marked the first time in my life that I felt unconditionally accepted for simply being me. I had moved light years beyond being a high school pariah.

And yet I never managed to transcend the indelible sense of estrangement that I felt as a child and teenager, and I continued to be plagued gnawing insecurities. I subconsciously thought that those insecurities would be quelled if I excelled as a funeral director, but, after excelling as a funeral director, I was still plagued by insecurities. Now I attempted to quell my insecurities by excelling as the proprietor of an escort service.

Although being a funeral director by day and a D.C. madam by night was very demanding, I nonetheless phoned my mother every night while I manned the phones, and I also made a trek to Williamson once a month. When I flew to Williamson, I generally departed early in the morning and returned in the evening. I managed to have dinner with Aunt Josephine about once a month too.

•••

I started to receive frequent calls from Paul Balach, who was the Secretary of Labor's personal liaison to the White House. Paul phoned me prolifically, and our chats evolved into relatively protracted conversations. He eventually invited me to lunch at Mr. Henry's, a Victorian pub and restaurant on Capitol Hill that attracts D.C. movers and shakers. Paul was tall, middle-aged, and overweight. He had thick, wavy black hair, and his face had fleshy jowls. Paul knocked back three or four screwdrivers as we ate lunch. He was naturally clumsy, and the screwdrivers exacerbated his clumsiness. During our first lunch, he knocked over a bottle of ketchup and spilled a glass of water. Despite his clumsiness, I found him to be a generous, kindhearted soul. He even gave me a pair of presidential cufflinks.

I sincerely liked Paul, and we started to regularly lunch at Mr. Henry's. I think Paul had major self-esteem issues, because he seemed to fall in love with every escort I sent to him. Paul was especially smitten by an escort named Michael Manos, and I discovered he bought Manos a car and lavished him with jewelry. Paul wasn't independently wealthy, and I just hated to see him being taken advantage of by an escort. I felt it was incumbent on me to convey to Paul that Manos didn't love him, but rather loved his money. My intervention, however, didn't assuage Paul's largesse, because he was so smitten by Manos.

The vast majority of the escorts I employed were absolute sweethearts, but unfortunately Paul had fallen in love with a nasty piece of work. Manos was svelte with blond hair and blue eyes, and he hailed from upstate New York. Before becoming an escort, Manos had worked at a Benetton clothing store, so his preppy apparel and his charming personality were quite disarming and even enchanting. He was a natural born salesman, and I think that he had the powers of persuasion to sell contraceptives to a convent.

Indeed, Manos certainly managed to con me. He initially requested to crash on my couch for a night or two, and that night or two turned into months. As I became increasingly aware of Manos bilking Paul, I told Manos that Paul was a friend of mine, and he should cease and desist bamboozling Paul into thinking that he loved him. Manos consented to quit conning Paul, but it was merely a ruse, because he eventually stole Paul's MasterCard and started forging his checks. When I found out about Manos' latest antics with Paul, I gave him the boot from my apartment and I fired him. Manos vowed to exact vengeance on me as he stormed out of my apartment. Following his departure, I realized that he had stolen my wallet. After I threatened to involve the police, Manos retuned my wallet three days later via a courier. But he would purloin my identity at a most inopportune time.

•••

I generally had extra escorts on call during the weekends because of my increased call volume on Friday and Saturday nights. But occasionally I found myself inundated by calls on weekday nights and didn't have the escorts to cover all of the calls. On those rare instances, I would personally respond to calls. One weekday night, I found myself responding to a call at Georgetown's Papermill Condos due to a shortage of escorts.

After exiting the elevator at the penthouse, I knocked on the caller's door. A short, heavy-set bald man cautiously cracked the door open and scrutinized me though a pair of thick, brown-framed glasses that significantly magnified his eyes. He then invited me into the spacious apartment, and we exchanged introductions. He introduced himself as Alan. His apartment offered a magnificent view of the Potomac River, and it was tastefully furnished. The coffee table in the living room was five feet in diameter and made of solid granite. The walls were adorned with photos of Alan and various presidents and congressmen. We sat down on his living room sofa, and he chopped up several lines of cocaine. After he partook of a line, he offered me a toot, but I demurred.

Although I found Alan to be a very intriguing, intelligent man, I sensed that he was smothered by loneliness. The following week, he invited me to Geppetto's, which is spacious restaurant in Bethesda, Maryland, specializing in Italian cuisine and Sicilian pizza, and I accepted his invitation. Alan was a lovely man, and a friendship gradually developed between us. We regularly met for lunch or dinner. Alan and I had only one sexual encounter, but he became a prolific client of my escort service, and his predilection was for boy-next-door types.

After I had routinely dined with Alan for approximately six months, I was following the 1988 presidential returns on television, and answering phones, when I discerned the inflection of a voice that was acutely familiar. I craned towards the television, and I noticed that the voice belonged to Alan Baron. I had no idea that the man I had befriended was, in fact, Democratic big-shot Alan Baron. At the time, he was the publisher of the *Baron Report*, a weekly newsletter on politics. Alan was also a political pundit for the *Wall Street Journal*, and he frequently appeared on *MacNeil/Lehrer NewsHour*. He even served a stint as the executive director of the Democratic National Committee. Despite all of Alan's worldly success and influential friends, I felt sorry from him, because he was such a lonely man.

A month or so after I met Alan Baron, I was fielding calls on a weekday night, and a prospective client phoned me from the Omni Hotel on Wisconsin Avenue. He requested an 18-year-old with minimal body hair and a slender swimmer's physique. I found his request to be disconcerting for a couple of reasons. First, he essentially sounded like he desired an underage boy, and, second, none of the escorts working that night remotely corresponded to his desires—except me—so I decided to visit the Omni Hotel.

I parked on Wisconsin Street, and I walked through the Omni's lobby to the elevator. Departing the elevator, I knocked on the gentleman's room. Congressman Barney Frank answered the door—he had given me a pseudonym over the phone. As we sat on the sofa in his hotel room, he pointed to an end table that had $200 in cash splayed on it. His gesture signified to me that he was seasoned veteran of escort etiquette. After I scooped up the money, he then started to hug and kiss me. Congressman Frank was extremely out of shape, and he had a very hairy body. I found my interaction with the congressman to be a rather dysphoric experience.

U.S. Representative Larry Craig from Idaho also became a frequent flyer of my escort service. Craig preferred escorts who were quite masculine with a plethora of body hair—bear types. Craig certainly bamboozled the conservative voters of Idaho who ultimately elected him to the U.S. Senate, where he developed quite a reputation for voting against gay legislation. Craig voted for a constitutional ban of same-sex marriage, and he voted against expanding hate crimes to include sexual orientation. In fact, the Human Rights Campaign, the nation's largest gay and lesbian civil rights organization, gave him a zero percent concerning his stance on gay-rights legislation. So Senator Larry Craig proved to be a major hypocrite.

In 2007, Senator Craig was arrested for lewd conduct in a restroom at the Minneapolis-St. Paul International Airport, because he attempted to pick up an undercover police officer in a bathroom stall. I was stunned to hear that Craig's repressed yet runaway libido compelled him to cruise for sex in an airport bathroom. Despite Craig's compulsive appetite for homosexual sex, as evinced by his soliciting sex in a public restroom, he had a nearly 30 year run as a U.S. congressman and senator in Washington, D.C.

Craig Spence's D.C. House

CHAPTER EIGHT

BLACKMAIL

I had been in business for a year or so when I answered the casket hotline. The caller said his name was Craig Spence, and I found him to be quite garrulous. Typically, the initial phone call placed to me by clients was brief, and they often provided a pseudonym, but Spence disclosed that he was a lobbyist who lived in D.C.'s upscale Kalorama neighborhood. He made a point of mentioning that he had a black MasterCard, which carried a $1 million line of credit. Spence then told me that he had bought two houses in the posh neighborhood, and built a corridor between the two. Spence said that he lived in one of the homes, and his "security" lived in the other home. He requested a young, boyish escort—18 or 19 years old.

I phoned Jimmy, and he sent an escort to Spence's home. Two hours later, Spence phoned again, requesting a second escort, which Jimmy quickly dispatched to his residence. At the time, I found my conversations with Spence extremely perplexing, and I will forever ruefully regret the day that he contacted me.

Spence started phoning me almost every day, and he spent up to $20,000 a month on escorts, becoming my most prolific and lucrative client. The vast sums he spent on escorts translated into well over 100 sessions a month. I was puzzled by his exorbitant expenditures, so I questioned the various escorts who had been dispatched to his residence about their respective encounters with Spence. Some described bacchanalian orgies. Other escorts who had one-on-one encounters with Spence described his penchant for extreme depravity. He was fond of being shackled, fettered, and whipped, and he also had a predilection for being beaten up and urinated on. Spence was certainly an enigma to me, because I sincerely wondered how he became so deranged. The revelations unfurled by the escorts who called on him prompted me to send only extremely seasoned escorts to his house.

I had been interacting with Spence over the phone for a couple of months when he invited me to his Kalorama home. Given the anecdotes that were conveyed to me by the escorts who had dealt with Spence face-to-face, I felt apprehensive when I drove to his home. As I slowly prowled down Wyoming Avenue, I noticed Spence's two-story brick home. Walking to the front door, I took a deep breath and rang the doorbell. A tall, muscular man in a pricy blue suit answered the door. He was in his early thirties, and he had a square, chiseled face, somber blue eyes, and dark brown hair.

After I introduced myself, he invited me into the marble foyer, and then shepherded me to a second floor office. An oriental rug rested on the office's marble floor, and intricately carved teakwood panels decorated the walls. As I was directed to a seat in front of Spence's desk, I glanced at the photographs on the walls. The photographs were quite formal, and they showed Spence standing next to various older men in suits. The only individuals I recognized in the photographs were Ronald Reagan and Bob Dole, and both were standing next to Spence with gaping smiles. I was slightly surprised that he didn't seem to have pictures of his family or family members.

Craig Spence sat behind an immense cherrywood desk, wearing an Edwardian-cut, plaid suit, white shirt, and black silk tie. Although Spence was in his forties, he had a youthful, blanched face. His thinning, sandy brown hair was parted to the left, and he had a well-groomed brown moustache. A pair of brown-framed designer glasses rested on the end of his nose, and he glanced upward, over his glasses, as he focused his icy blue eyes on me. He leaned forward in his chair and introduced himself without extending his hand. Spence certainly didn't come across as the reprobate described by the escorts, but rather he appeared to be a refined gentleman.

After Spence's perfunctory introduction, he launched into a longwinded soliloquy. His initial remarks were a resume of sorts: He said that he was a lobbyist as well as a consultant for various interests in Japan and the health care industry. Spence then told me that he had "friends" who were perched at the pinnacle of power. He emphatically stated that he held the reins to omnipotence, and he had the ability to make a "life altering" phone call. He repeatedly reiterated that he could make "life altering" phone calls.

Spence said that his security force consisted of off-duty Secret Service agents. The man who had ushered me into Spence's office stood just outside the office door. When Spence called for him, he quickly skipped into the room. After Spence told him to show me his credentials, he whipped out his Secret Service badge and credentials, which I scrutinized. Spence then gestured for him to leave the office, and he followed Spence's orders like a trained poodle.

After Spence concluded expounding on his power and connections, he discussed my role in his grand vision. He made it crystal clear that my escorts were interacting with the most powerful men in the country, so the caliber of escort was imperative to him. He required the highest quality escorts, who were punctual and impeccably dressed. He required escorts who were articulate and appeared to be college graduates. He required that I diligently screen and qualify escorts to meet his lofty standards. Spence barked out his demands as if he were barking out orders in Marine boot camp, and he emphasized that it was a privilege for me to provide him with escorts.

Spence struck me as extremely smart and also very manipulative. He was a morass of arrogance and extreme narcissism that I had never encountered before. He indeed believed that he resided at the center of the universe, and I was merely a pawn in his grandiose game of chess. Spence certainly didn't impart a warm and fuzzy feeling during our initial meeting. In Shakespeare's *King Lear*, Gloucester and Edgar have a dialogue, and Edgar declares that the "Prince of Darkness is a gentleman." As I departed Spence's home that day, I felt like I had just met the Prince of Darkness.

Spence continued to phone me almost everyday, and about a month after our initial meeting he again summoned me to his home. I was met at the door by one his security personnel, who escorted me into the living room, which was beautifully furnished and decorated. The living room had a glossy, hardwood floor that was adorned with exquisite oriental rugs, and its walls were garnished with high-priced neo-classical paintings. His living room also had towering bookshelves.

Spence and an African-American man in his forties were reclined on the living room's chocolate colored sofa, and I was directed to a leather chair that was adjacent to the sofa. Spence was casually dressed in designer jeans and a pink Polo shirt, and, after I sat down, he introduced me to Larry King, his African-American friend. King was rather obese, and he wore a resplendent navy blue suit that I thought was either an Armani or Brioni. He had meticulously coifed straight black hair and a trim goatee. His large-framed designer glasses had tinted lenses that partially obscured his beady, darting eyes. A thick gold chain draped his neck, and he had a bulky gold ring that was encrusted by diamonds. King exuded a pomp and flashiness that even surpassed that of Spence.

Spence gave me a chilly reception as King looked on with a sinister smile. Spence then started our meeting by excoriating me, because one of my escorts had belatedly arrived at his home. I explained to him that I had taken a three-day vacation, and I wasn't able to tend to the phone with my customary alacrity. Spence snapped that if he thought I needed a vacation, he would send me on a vacation. As Spence excoriated me, he was hunched over a china bowl on the living room's large, circular crystal coffee table. The china bowl was brimming with cocaine, and he was dipping a gold coke spoon into it. Spence eventually offered me a toot of coke, but I declined.

After Spence had taken two or three toots of coke, he started to chatter about his exalted status and clout—specks of cocaine littered his mustache. King also chimed in about his exalted status and clout too. I felt like Spence was putting on a show for King, but King wasn't an individual who acquiesced to being out-boasted. They pumped themselves up like cartoonish parade balloons that were on the brink of bursting. Although I found their boasts to be almost comedic, I refrained from laughing.

King then made a number of disclosures that I found to be absolutely bizarre. He revealed that he and Spence operated an interstate pedophile network that flew children from coast-to-coast. King also discussed that he and Spence had a clientele of powerful pedophiles who actually took pleasure in murdering children. In fact, King seemed to be obsessed with the subject of murdering children. I sincerely thought that I was talking to a pair of psychotics on the run from a psychiatric hospital.

After Spence and King conversed about their rarified statuses and their extreme pedophilic perversities, Spence shifted gears and started to sincerely inquire about my life. He asked where I was born and where I attended college. He then questioned me about the particulars of my escort service. In the context of our earlier discussion, Spence's questions seemed like non-sequiturs to me.

Though I answered Spence's questions truthfully, I was uncertain about the motivation for his inquiries, because Spence struck me as an individual who generally had a self-centered, utilitarian reason for every action. I also found it nearly impossible to believe that Spence's seismic narcissism made him constitutionally capable of taking a sincere interest in me. I thought that either he had a duplicitous reason for plying me with seemingly heartfelt questions or I was witnessing a miracle tantamount to the parting of the Red Sea. As Spence inquired about my life, King sipped his drink and was ominously silent, but an unnerving smile was etched on his face.

When Spence finished quizzing me about my life, he stood up and gestured for me to accompany him. I stood up and followed him. King remained seated on the sofa. Spence walked toward a large mirror that was situated on living room wall, and opened a closet door that was in the corner of his living room. He popped open a secret panel that was embedded in the closet, and he stepped into a small room that was behind the mirror.

I cautiously paused at the threshold of the closet, but Spence waved his right hand, signifying that I should follow him into the surreptitious room. The mirror on the living room wall was, in fact, a two-way mirror, and the room had a video camera on a tripod that was pointed toward the living room and also a wall of video monitors. Spence leaned over one of the video monitors, and, after tapping a few of its buttons, he replayed the concluding minutes of our conversation. At that moment, I felt shrink-wrapped by cellophane, and I found it difficult to breath.

As I silently stared at the monitor, Spence casually smiled and explained to me that his entire home was bugged for clandestine surveillance, and "CIA operatives" had installed the concealed video cameras throughout his house. He couldn't help himself from crowing that his surveillance equipment was state-of-the-art, and the camera that captured our conversations was embedded in the living room's thermostat.

Spence then divulged that he blackmailed the rich and powerful. I remained stunned and speechless as I watched myself discussing my life and escort service on the video monitor, but, after a few minutes, I started to swell with anger. However, I didn't express my anger to Spence, because, at that moment, I was undeniably frightened of him, and I'm also not a confrontational person. Once Spence had flaunted his blackmail equipment, he dispensed a grave threat about the "consequences" if I uttered nary a word relating to his concealed cameras. He then dismissed me.

I walked out of his house in a state of shock. My mouth was parched, and an adrenal chill coursed through my body. A montage of the video footage of me discussing my life relentlessly overwhelmed my thoughts as I drove home that night. I was utterly dumbfounded by King's disclosures too. I have to confess that I was in a state of denial about King's revelations, because they were so bizarre. I found it hard to believe that people could be such unequivocal monsters. But Spence had videotaped me discussing the particulars of my life and my escort service, so I was now susceptible to blackmail. I no longer viewed Spence as a mere client—I felt he controlled me. Indeed, he started to tell the escorts I sent to his home that I worked for him. The escort service had started out as a carefree venture that was enjoyable and exciting, but Spence had imbued it with a sinister gravitas.

Spence's unbounded egocentricity and bravado aside, it was quite evident to me that he had stratospheric connections, so I felt compelled to remain mute about our second meeting. I liken my interactions with Spence to family, sit-down dinners at the Vinson household with my father: I didn't think it was a recipe for a happy ending.

Spence continued to phone me almost everyday for escorts. And three weeks following our second meeting, he once more summoned me to his home. Driving to Spence's home that night, I was fraught with anxiety and unsure of the next surprise he planned to spring on me. One of Spence's security personnel greeted me at the door, and he directed me to the living room.

Spence was in the midst of hosting an unbridled orgy that had the ornate trappings of an inaugural ball. Magnums of Dom Pérignon and china bowls brimming with cocaine were scattered throughout Spence's living room. I think the majority of the participants were military personnel, because military uniforms were littered on the floor and strewn over furniture. A three-star general who was fully clothed sat next to Spence on the sofa. He was heavyset and around six feet tall. He had gray hair and distinguished facial features, and he nonchalantly conversed with Spence as if they were seated in a D.C. restaurant. Spence was wearing an Edwardian-cut pastel plaid suit, a white shirt, and a blue tie.

The orgy consisted of approximately thirty people who were at various stages of disrobing, and they were also tangled up in various sexual acts, ranging from oral sex to intercourse. Six or seven of the male escorts worked for me, but I also noticed six or seven women in their early twenties who were also escorts. Four nude men in their twenties surrounded a very attractive female escort who was on the floor squatted on all fours. One of the men entered her from behind as she performed oral on a second man. Two men looked on, masturbating while waiting their turn to be with her.

I seated myself next to Spence, on the same chair I had sat on during our previous meeting, and he was quite congenial to me. I think he wanted me to behold one of his bacchanalian orgies in full bloom, and that was the primary impetus for him summoning me to his home. As Spence occasionally surveyed the orgy with a smile and a seeming sense of accomplishment, he and the general discussed a health care interest of theirs in Japan. Spence was a consultant for Becton, Dickinson & Company, which manufactures a gamut of medical supplies, devices, laboratory equipment and diagnostic products, but I was unable to discern if his conversation with the general related to Becton, Dickinson & Company.

Although Spence came across as friendly, I felt extremely uncomfortable and guarded, because I was cognizant of the fact that everybody in the living room was probably being videotaped. I conversed with Spence for about ten or fifteen minutes, and I politely excused myself. Driving home that night, I reflected on the orgy. The male and female escorts were treated as if they were merely meat, and I felt utter disgust. My disgust was compounded by the fact that the orgy was most likely being videotaped. The night's sordid events weren't exactly what I had planned for my life.

Spence summoned me to his home a couple of weeks following our third meeting. Yet again, I was greeted by one of his security personnel who ushered me into the living room. Spence was sitting on the living room sofa by himself, wearing beige khakis and a light blue button down shirt. He was hunched over the china bowl on the living room's coffee table, tooting cocaine with his gold coke spoon.

Between toots of cocaine, Spence expressed his irritation with the performance of an escort. He elaborated on the hefty sums he spent on escorts, and he snapped that he expected every escort sent to his home to meet his exalted expectations. He reiterated that I was privileged to have him as a client. Once more, I was guarded about my disclosures due to his concealed cameras.

After Spence berated me for the performance of an escort, he nonchalantly mentioned enchanting an escort with a late night excursion of the White House. When Spence finished discussing the White House tour, he dismissed me with a wave of his arm as he took a toot of coke. I had great difficulty believing that Spence actually arranged an after hours excursion of the White House for an escort, so I asked the escort in question about it. He confirmed that Spence pulled up to the White House gate, and Secret Service personnel instantly waved him through the gate.

Since my second meeting with Spence, I had ruminated about Spence's disclosure that CIA operatives had installed his blackmail equipment. When Spence initially disclosed that statement to me, I was too stunned to attempt to discern if it were true. And over the ensuing weeks, I vacillated between credulity and incredulity. But after sitting next to a three-star general in the midst of an orgy that was most likely being videotaped, and having an escort confirm Spence's after hours tour of the White House, I had a tendency to believe that he might be telling the truth, because, after all, his equipment was state-of-the-art and also because of the power he wielded. I thought John Q. Citizen would have great difficulties acquiring such high-tech equipment, and I didn't think a single individual could pull off everything Spence managed to pull off. I started to believe, and subsequent events confirmed, that Spence's enterprise had the blessing of officials poised at the pinnacle of the federal government.

•••

The day Spence introduced himself to me on the casket hotline irrevocably altered the trajectory of my life, and, over the years, I've struggled to understand the phenomenon of Craig Spence. Prior to 1989, Spence seemed to be immune to bad press despite the fact that he was an outright sociopath. A 1983 *New York Times* profile of Spence, "Have Names, Will Open Right Door," described him as "something of a mystery man." The *New York Times* profile noted Spence's puzzling personality and stratospheric social connections, but it didn't offer an explanation of his wealth and power.

Spence rarely discussed his personal life with me, and he occasionally discussed his familial roots, so it's difficult to comprehend how he accumulated the juice and guile to blackmail the elite and influential. Spence occasionally mentioned that he was an only child who descended from Boston bluebloods, but I've read that he was most likely born in upstate New York. It's also been reported that he attended Syracuse University before enrolling in Boston College. A former Boston College classmate told a reporter that Spence covered his tuition with student loans, which almost certainly excludes him from the ranks of Boston bluebloods. He graduated from Boston College in 1963 with a degree in Communications and Broadcasting.

After his college graduation, Spence started out as a press assistant for Massachusetts' governor, and then he became a press secretary for the Massachusetts' state speaker. Spence eventually moved to New York City, landing employment as a correspondent for WCBS, New York City's CBS affiliate. In 1969, he made the leap to ABC as a Vietnam correspondent.

Spence was a conundrum among his fellow Vietnam correspondents. It wasn't uncommon for him to disappear for weeks at a time, and one of his fellow correspondents even commented on his ability to glean covert information: "Craig always looked like he had learned something that no one else knew."

After leaving ABC and Vietnam in 1970, Spence relocated to Tokyo. While in Tokyo, it's been reported that he supported himself as a freelance radio correspondent throughout the mid-1970s. Spence then somehow reinvented himself by forging a business relationship with Japanese politician Motoo Shiina. Shiina was in the Japanese parliament, and he wasn't a political hack of the five-and-dime variety. He came from an aristocratic family that had primed him for political eminence. Shiina's father, Etsusaburo, was an affluent businessman and Japanese powerbroker, who had been appointed to key positions within the Japanese cabinet.

Spence once dispensed a rather candid remark to a reporter about his relationship with Motoo Shiina. "Motoo's father, Etsusaburo, who was a great man, asked me to help his son, who he saw as playboy." I find Spence's comment to be rather ironic, because if I were a father grooming my son for political prominence, and he had a runaway libido that might hinder his political promise, Spence would be the last person in the world I would request to help him.

When Motoo Shiina and Spence teamed up, Shiina was the president of the Policy Study Group (PSG), a Tokyo-based venture that was subsidized by monies from both the Japanese private and public sectors. PSG's primary purpose was to facilitate Japanese business interests by creating alliances among Japanese businessmen and influential Americans and captains of industry.

In 1979, Spence became the "overseas representative" for PSG. Shiina provided Spence with a hefty salary and coughed up $345,000 for Spence to buy his Kalorama home. The Kalorama home was to serve as a residence for Spence and also be "Shiina's embassy" in D.C. and the American headquarters of PSG. In 1983, the honeymoon between Spence and Shiina abruptly ended. Shiina demanded that Spence vacate his Kalorama digs, but Spence refused. In court papers, Shiina stated the following about Spence's home: "I was advised that staying at the house while Spence was there could be damaging to my reputation." Four years later, I came to the same conclusion as Shiina.

Spence, however, had leverage on Shiina, because the money Shiina transferred to purchase the Kalorama home had been transferred into the United States illegally via Hong Kong, so Spence's lawyers eventually forced Shiina to back down, and they ultimately worked out an arrangement: Spence would compensate Shiina for the home when he decided to sell it. So Shiina was essentially Spence's first blackmail victim—at least on record. If Spence were willing to extort one of the most powerful men in Japan, he wouldn't think twice about blackmailing a mortician from West Virginia.

Craig Spence

Chapter Nine

The Prince of Darkness

S ince my second face-to-face encounter with Spence, I had truly come to look upon him as the Prince of Darkness. I assumed that every visit I made to his home was recorded, and I also felt that he had the power and connections to crush me. But I managed to provide him with escorts that were a facsimile of his exalted expectations, and we ultimately arrived at a détente of sorts. Although I had to regularly assuage his outbreaks of grandiosity and insanity, he continued to spend up to $20,000 a month on escorts.

The worries and anxieties posed by Spence notwithstanding, my escort service continued to flourish. But the rising volume of calls proved to be a problem for Jimmy. He had become increasingly dysfunctional due to the fact that he had started popping Dilaudid like jellybeans. I repeatedly attempted to intervene, but his love for Dilaudid had even eclipsed his love for elephants.

My expanding business and Jimmy's burgeoning dysfunction prompted me to hire a second person, Travis, to operate the phones. Jimmy had introduced me to Travis. He was a tall, thin 21-year-old who had thick blond hair and gentle blue eyes. Travis was strikingly handsome, but he didn't have the one-on-one people skills to thrive as an escort. But he had a simpatico personality, so I gave him an opportunity to work the phones. He excelled at talking to clients and also directing the appropriate escorts to them. Travis generally answered the phones after 1:00 A.M., when I folded for the night, until Jimmy showed up the next day. At that point, Jimmy's hours had become extremely elastic.

On a Saturday afternoon, after I had lunched at the National Air and Space Museum, I was sitting in my apartment, watching television, answering phones, when I received a call from a man named "Tony" who said he was a friend of Craig Spence. Tony requested to meet with me, and I suggested that we rendezvous at a restaurant or at his home, but he replied that he would drop by my apartment. Although I had never disclosed the whereabouts of my apartment to Spence, Tony said he knew exactly where I lived.

Within in an hour, I heard the roar of motorcycles. Peering out my living room window, I noticed three men parking their motorcycles in front of my apartment building. I then heard a heavy rap on my apartment door. I answered the door, and Tony introduced himself. He was flanked by two hulking men in their early thirties.

Tony was in his mid-thirties. He had a swarthy complexion and jet-black hair. He cradled a black motorcycle helmet in his left arm and wore a black leather jacket and black leather chaps. His bearded face almost had a cubist appearance due to multiple cosmetic surgeries. Cosmetic surgery had significantly reduced his nose to a mere wrinkle that seemed disproportionate to his face. He appeared to be Italian, but he had the same icy blue eyes as Spence that sent a shiver down my spine.

The two men who accompanied Tony were stunningly handsome, muscle laden, and wearing black jogging suits. The man on Tony's right was about 6'2" with blue eyes and blond hair, and the taller man on his left had blue eyes and blond hair. They had blank, subdued facial expressions.

I had a flash of intuition that I had seen Tony before, and, as I momentarily gazed at his face, my memory of him quickly congealed. I recalled seeing Tony on my third visit to Spence's house—he had been one of the orgy's participants. I also recalled walking out of a Benetton clothing store near the intersection of Wisconsin Avenue and P Street shortly after my third visit to Spence's home, and seeing Tony and the two hulking men leaning against a wall, staring at me. I distinctly remembered their unwarranted attention. We exchanged glances, but I felt intimidated by them, so I didn't utter a word. I promptly came to the uncomfortable realization that Tony was cognizant of where I lived, because he had probably been following me.

Tony seated himself in the chair in front of my desk and reclined as if he owned the apartment. The men who accompanied him seated themselves on the sofa. Tony's cohorts were silent, but he was quite talkative. Although Tony appeared to be quite masculine, he had a high-pitched voice, and he spoke with sweeping gesticulations that were slightly effeminate. I discerned that he was most likely gay, but he was hard-boiled gay. Indeed, he's the most hard-boiled gay man I've ever met. He came across as seemingly omniscient and intimidating.

Tony initially mentioned that he too ran a gay escort service, and he had catered to Craig Spence for years. He said that he "worked closely" with Spence, and his "blessing" was the primary reason I had acquired Spence as a client. Tony, like Spence, also discussed his extensive power and connections, even though he didn't infuse his braggadocio with the grandiosity of Spence. Tony then looked me straight into the eye and snapped that I should be weary about ever crossing him, because he had the technology to overload my phone lines and render my phones inoperable and the government connections to shut me down at his whim. He also mentioned that he was aware of my day job at the Chambers Funeral Homes, which I found rather distressing.

Tony ended our conversation with a friendly request that, at the time, I found to be perplexing. He said that he didn't have the ability to process credit cards, and he inquired if I had the means to process credit cards. After I replied that I would look into the possibility, Tony concluded our meeting. Since I thought that he and Spence were most likely in cahoots, I thought I should attempt to placate his request. In hindsight, it's apparent to me that Tony's request was a disingenuous ploy.

The following week, I phoned my mother, and I told her that I had started an entertainment business. I inquired if she could process credit cards for me through her ambulance company. Tony phoned shortly after I talked to my mother, and we met at Annie's Paramount Steakhouse, which is near DuPont Circle. When I arrived, Tony and his two brutes were seated at a table in the back of the steakhouse, sipping drinks. Tony's brutes were again wearing black jogging suits, but the tops of their jogging suits were strategically unzipped, exposing their shoulder holsters and guns. I was taken aback as I briefly stared at their guns. My glance subsequently grazed their faces, and each flashed a menacing grin.

After I ordered a coke, Tony inquired if I had acquired the means to process credit cards. I gave him an affirmative nod. Tony responded with a rare smile, and he handed me a dozen credit card vouchers. He then knocked back the rest of his drink and stood up. His brutes then stood up and silently followed him out of the restaurant.

Shortly after my second meeting with Tony, Spence summoned me to his home. One of his security personnel directed me to the vacant living room, and I sat in my customary chair. A few minutes later, Spence and Tony walked into the living room. They seemed to be in a jovial mood as they sat on the sofa. Spence initiated the conversation by saying that Tony was his right hand man, and Tony had taken care of "a lot of business" for him over the years. Apparently, Spence was aware of my newfound ability to process credit cards, because he piped he would "fix any problems" I encountered. Although my feelings at the time were amorphous, I nonetheless had a vague intuition that I was like a lamb being led to slaughter.

At the end of our meeting, Spence invited me to a Capitol Hill party, but I declined. And during our subsequent meetings, he invited me to various events and parties, and I declined those invitations too. I didn't have a desire to meet Spence's powerbroker friends due to the fact that I thought Spence was wicked, and I felt that soirées among Spence's friends would be awkward and cumbersome. Spence eventually started to become miffed that I didn't have an inclination to attend events and parties with him. He repeatedly told me that I should ingratiate myself to his powerbroker friends, but I repeatedly evaded his invitations by voicing various obligations at the funeral home.

•••

I started to meet with Tony on an almost weekly basis. We usually met at Annie's on weekday nights, and Tony would invariably arrive before me. Tony and his two brutes would be sitting at a table in the back of the restaurant, nursing drinks. The two brutes always accompanied Tony—we never met one-on-one. When we rendezvoused, Tony provided me with a new batch of signed credit card vouchers to process, and I would hand him the cash from the previous batch.

I didn't feel quite right about my mother processing credit cards, so I quickly asked Robert to create a merchant account through the Chambers Funeral Homes to process credit cards. The merchant account that we used was called Professional Services, so my clients who used credit cards were billed for various funeral accessories, and Robert received a 20 percent cut of the revenues.

Tony eventually provided me with the name and phone number of a credit card processing company in Miami, Florida. He said that a friend of his worked for the company, and his friend would walk me through the process of setting up a merchant account. When I phoned the company, Tony's "friend" was gracious and helpful as he facilitated the creation of a merchant account for me. I found this chain of events extremely puzzling. I wondered why Tony hadn't used his friend to establish his own merchant account.

During our weekly meetings, I occasionally asked Tony for information on clients whose behaviors perplexed me. Tony would run a complete background check on the requested individual, providing me with the individual's home address, his place of employment, his income, etc. For example, I had a client named Vernon Houk, who periodically holed up in D.C. hotel and ordered up to five escorts a day, and he was also into unprotected sex. Tony told me that Houk was the director of the Center for Environmental Heath at the Centers for Disease Control and Prevention. I was slightly perplexed that Houk was a high flyer at the CDC, but yet he was so into unprotected sex.

Charles Dutcher was another client whose behavior perplexed me, due the exorbitant amounts of money he spent on escorts. Tony relayed to me that Dutcher was the former associate director of presidential personnel in the Reagan administration.

Tony had access to such information well before the advent of Google, which led me to believe that he was affiliated with the government or rather some dark pocket of the government.

Spence later told me that Tony had a shadowy CIA affiliation, and he was part and parcel of Spence's blackmail enterprise. Spence also told me that Tony's brutes had been Special Forces operatives. Tony, however, was like a phantom to me, even though he led me to believe that he was affiliated with the government. I made inquiries about his identity, but I never managed to learn even his last name. Like Spence, Tony frequently alluded to his power and connections, although, unlike Spence, he said very little that was definitive.

Spence could be quite candid about his blackmail enterprise and occasionally provided the names of his targets, but Tony never discussed blackmail with me. However, given the events that later unfolded, I've come to believe that Tony was part and parcel of Spence's blackmail enterprise. After we had met five or six times, Tony started alluding to contract hits that he had carried out. I found Tony's disclosures to have an incomprehensibility that rivaled that of Spence and, for that matter, King. Following his disclosures about contract hits, his brutes and the guns that they toted made me all the more frightened of them.

Shortly after Tony abruptly barged into my life, I had a suspicion that my phones were tapped. As I talked to clients and escorts, I heard incessant clicking sounds. I ultimately noticed a large box van that was parked across the street from my apartment. Most of the men who skirted in and out of the van wore blue industrial overalls and hard hats, but I occasionally spotted men wearing suits shuffling in and out of the van.

•••

According to my escorts, Spence had graduated from tooting cocaine to smoking crack, and I started to find our interactions to be increasing onerous due to his escalating madness. Spence was never the quintessence of sanity, but, prior to his crack addiction, he maintained a semblance of sanity that made our interactions slightly rational. After his crack addiction, however, I cringed every time we met face-to-face. His physical and emotion deterioration were striking too. He started to appear gaunt and sickly, and he became increasingly paranoid. He repeatedly remarked that his security personnel were out to murder him.

One night he summoned me to his home, where I found him and Larry King sitting on the sofa. I was essentially blackmailed during my first meeting with Spence and King, and I found my subsequent meetings with the tandem quite unpleasant, because they attempted to coerce me into ensnaring children for them. King had previously mentioned that he flew children into D.C., and the escorts I employed confirmed that minors were in attendance at Spence's orgies.

Despite my earlier state of denial, I had come to the horrifying conclusion that Spence and King operated an interstate pedophile network for their powerbroker cronies. But I absolutely refused to aid and abet their abuse of children, despite Spence's potential to blackmail me or perhaps even kill me.

As we sat in Spence's living room, Spence and King once more broached the subject of me procuring children for them, but they started becoming extremely aggressive. Although I emphatically told them that I wouldn't pander children, their demands escalated to an inexorable crescendo: Spence and King finally demanded that I pluck destitute children off the streets of D.C. and deliver the children to them. After I realized that they weren't willing to cease and desist about the issue, I excused myself and walked out of Spence's home.

Leaving Spence's house that night, I decided I needed to extricate myself from Spence, King, and Tony. Spence's crack addiction had made him extremely irrational, and pandering children was a line that I absolutely refused to cross. I also never felt comfortable dealing with Tony, and his request that I process credit cards never made sense to me. I decided to quit providing Spence with escorts and processing Tony's credit card vouchers, so I stopped returning their calls. Every time Spence or Tony's numbers came up on the casket hotline's caller ID or on the T1, I wouldn't answer the call. Spence had seemingly infinite resources, and I optimistically thought that he would simply start using a different escort service, but I was regrettably wrong.

I quickly discovered that my Faustian pact with Spence and Tony didn't have an exit clause. As I departed my apartment for work one morning, I noticed Tony and his two brutes across the street leering at me. Needless to say, I was terrified. Departing work, I again spotted the trio across the street from the funeral home.

Driving home that night, I repeatedly peered in my rearview mirror, but I didn't notice them following me. However, when I returned to my apartment, Jimmy told me that the phones had been malfunctioning. Tony had computerized automatic dialers that repeatedly dialed my main numbers and overloaded my lines. He sent my escorts out on bogus calls too. Jimmy and Travis had also received death threats as they answered the phones throughout the day. I had never edified them about the ominous partnership between Spence and Tony, but now I felt it was incumbent on me to explain Spence and Tony and their rarified caliber of psychopathology. I told Jimmy and Travis that I wouldn't begrudge them if they said farewell to the escort service. But both opted not to quit.

My primary phone numbers were down for the balance of the night, so calls sporadically trickled into the T1. As I watched television, I heard intermittent pounding on my windows, which provoked petrifying surges of terror. I crawled into my bed around 11:00 P.M. I attempted to sleep, but my nerves were too frayed, and I stared at my bedroom's ceiling for an hour or so. Just as I started to cross the threshold of sleep, the deafening blasts of gunshots were discharged outside my bedroom window.

The next day, I again noticed Tony and his brutes parked outside the funeral home. Throughout the day, I was a nervous wreck as I counseled a couple of families about their upcoming funeral arrangements. I attempted to maintain a calm exterior to the bereaved, even though I felt utterly exhausted, and I couldn't prevent myself from ruminating about my own upcoming funeral arrangements.

I made it back to my apartment around 6:00 P.M., and Jimmy told me that the phones were again malfunctioning. Jimmy left my apartment around 7:00 P.M., and, a few minutes after his departure, I heard a knock on the door. I thought Jimmy was knocking on the door, because he was prone to forgetfulness. When I opened the door, Tony's two brutes barged into my apartment. One knocked me down, and they proceeded to punch holes in the wall, upend furniture, break my apartment's windows, and rip drawers from the desk. They were like cyborgs programmed for Armageddon. I thought that Tony's brutes had been ordered to kill me, and I was absolutely mortified. As they demolished my apartment, I lunged towards the phone and dialed 911.

A few minutes into the melee, Tony casually walked into my apartment, smoking a cigarette. I had the phone's receiver in my right hand, and he quickly realized that I had called the police. He told me that I could either deal with him and Spence or die. After Tony dispensed his *to be or not to be*, he and his two brutes nonchalantly strolled out of my apartment. I had come to believe that Spence and Tony were pure malevolence, and, as I surveyed my demolished apartment, my beliefs had been incontrovertibly confirmed.

My own, private apocalypse had commenced.

Lawrence E. King, Jr.

CHAPTER TEN

IN THE EYE OF A HURRICANE

I was emotionally tattered and threadbare for weeks after Tony and his brutes demolished my apartment. My escort service had started out as a blithe, carefree adventure, but it had morphed into a larger than life leviathan that was beyond my control. I had created a Frankenstein, and I was impotent to guide its course. I could only sit by and watch as it controlled me.

I was a victim of my own success and over my head. I felt I couldn't turn to law enforcement, and I also felt that walking away wasn't an option either, because Tony would invariably hunt me down and kill me. I reluctantly decided to start dealing Spence and Tony once more, because I had come to believe that my self-preservation dictated that I didn't have a choice in the matter. But Spence never again insisted that I provide him with children.

As my escort service started spiraling out of my control, Robert began to experience trouble with his family, even though they weren't aware of our credit card arrangement. Although Robert went through the motions of being a heterosexual, I think his family had a mounting awareness of his secret life, because his father treated him like a second-class citizen. Robert and his family eventually reached a critical mass of irreconcilable differences, and they fired him. Robert and his wife and children had been living in a home that was owned by the funeral home. Following his termination, he purchased a house in Upper Marlboro, Maryland. After Robert found himself in the ranks of the unemployed, the credit cards I furnished him became his primary source of income.

Robert's father and brothers then pressured me to side with them against Robert, but Robert had become my closest friend, and I wouldn't disparage him. The pressure to take sides in the Chambers' family squabble became too distressing for me, and I eventually tendered my resignation to the funeral home. Though I had felt a calling to be a funeral director since I was child, my escort service had mutated into such a burdensome knot of complexities that resigning from the Chambers Funeral Homes actually came as a relief.

Shortly after Tony and his brutes ransacked my apartment, I rented a two-story, colonial house on 34th Place. The house's first floor had a spacious living room, dining room, and kitchen, and the second floor had three bedrooms. I settled in the master bedroom, and Jimmy and his copious collection of elephants moved into the second bedroom. I was concerned about Jimmy's escalating dysfunction, and I thought I had the potential to help him if he were in close proximity to me. I converted the third bedroom, which overlooked a second-story deck, into an office. Although I operated my escort service out of my new office, I didn't relinquish my apartment on New Hampshire Avenue. I left a phone system in the New Hampshire apartment, and Travis regularly answered phones from the apartment.

I attempted to make my relocation as clandestine as possible, so I opted not to move furniture from my apartment into the house, prompting a shopping spree at Ethan Allen. The 34th Place house was on a quiet cul-de-sac, and I had deluded myself into thinking the move would enhance my safety, even though in my heart of hearts I was cognizant of the fact that Tony and Spence would find me wherever I resurfaced. And unfortunately moving into the house didn't assuage the ubiquitous state of terror that had descended on me.

Around the time I started renting the house on 34th Place, Spence sold his Kalorama home, and relocated to a pair of condominiums on Massachusetts Avenue. The condominiums he purchased were side-by-side. Initially, he lived in one of the condominiums, and his security personnel lived in the adjacent condominium. After a few months, however, his security personnel vacated their condominium.

By that time, Spence was freefalling in the throes of crack addiction, and he had become an utter lunatic. Whatever shadowy, sub rosa network that had floated his lavish lifestyle and his security detail had clearly rescinded its backing, because Spence was in the midst of major financial difficulties. He no longer had the resources to spend $20,000 a month on escorts. Indeed, he had difficulties financing escorts solely for himself. Spence began phoning me numerous times throughout the course of a day, demanding that I comp him escorts.

When Spence sold his Kalorama home, my contacts with Tony started to wane too. Tony then suddenly vanished from my life just as suddenly as he had appeared. His various phone numbers were abruptly disconnected, and I never heard from him again. I was perplexed by Tony's vanishing act and also by Spence's harsh reversal of fortune. Although I felt a tremendous sense of relief when Tony receded from my life, I couldn't help myself from wondering if those events had foreboding implications for me.

••••

In January 1989, I received a puzzling phone call from a woman who worked for the Government Accounting Office. A patron of my escort service, Donald Gregg, had wracked up recurrent credit card charges for funeral accessories with his government-issued MasterCard, and the GAO employee had numerous questions about the charges. I was caught off guard by her questions, so I was uncertain of the appropriate response. I ultimately advised her that the charges were of a personal nature, and I suggested that she contact Donald Gregg. Right after the GAO contacted me, I phoned Spence and told him about the particulars of the call. He replied that he would be in touch.

Donald Gregg wasn't an average, run-of-the-mill government apparatchik. He had been a CIA agent for 31 years, and he played an integral role in the Phoenix Program, a nefarious CIA initiative that slaughtered over 25,000 South Vietnamese who were in many cases mistakenly thought to be collaborating with North Vietnam. When Gregg was soliciting gay escorts from me with his government issued MasterCard, he served as Vice President George H.W. Bush's national security advisor.

In 1983, Gregg had a secret meeting with CIA agent Felix Rodriguez and Vice President Bush in the White House, where the trio hatched a covert scheme to provide military aid to the Contras in Nicaragua, which ultimately morphed into Iran-Contra. CIA agent Rodriguez, too, had an infamous reputation, because he had been a cog in the dark machinations of the Phoenix Program, and he also helped hunt down Che Guevara in Bolivia and pilfered the watch from the dead Guevara as a trophy. Gregg and George H.W. Bush were old friends, and after the latter became president, he appointed Gregg to be the United States Ambassador to South Korea. So Gregg was someone that the Bush I administration felt inclined to protect from the fact that he procured gay escorts on the government dime.

Craig Spence hinted to the *Washington Times* that Donald Gregg had arranged his late night tours of the White House, but Gregg vehemently repudiated Spence's allegations as "absolute bull." Indeed, Gregg didn't seem to hold Spence in high esteem. "It disturbs me that he can reach a slimy hand out of the sewer to grab me by the ankle like this," Gregg said of Spence. In the article, Gregg said that he had met Spence only once, but, given the events that subsequently unfolded, I'm inclined to believe that Spence and Gregg had more than one contact.

Three weeks or so following the phone call from the GAO, Spence summoned me to his condominium. I hadn't seen Spence in two months, and I was shocked by his physical deterioration. He was emaciated, and his complexion was ashen. I later learned that in addition to a crack addiction, he had contracted AIDS. After Spence ushered me into his house, he motioned to a settee that was in his living room. As I sat down, Spence seated himself on his chocolate sofa next to man in his late fifties, who had balding black hair and brown, round-framed glasses. He wore a blue, pinstripe suit, white shirt, and a red tie. A miniature U.S. flag was pinned on his lapel. Spence introduced the man to me by his name and also disclosed his title. He was in the cabinet of George H.W. Bush. I feel that the Bush administration had decided to pull out a big gun to eradicate any traces of Gregg's affinity for gay escorts, because Gregg had been so instrumental in Iran-Contra and because he was en route to becoming the United States Ambassador to South Korea.

Spence had dropped the name of the cabinet member months earlier, when he revealed that he routinely provided him with adolescent boys. At the time Spence dropped his name and his perverse predications, I thought his disclosure broached incomprehensible, and I was fairly skeptical of it. But on the other hand, the vast majority of Spence's illicit activities seemed incomprehensible to me until I actually witnessed them.

Our conversation focused on the GAO conundrum, and Spence and his "friend" quickly cut to the chase. They told me to write a letter to the GAO detailing blood studies I had conducted on behalf of Gregg. They explained that my occupation as a mortician would be a satisfactory guise for the letter. I felt that I was potentially being set up for GAO embezzlement charges, and I balked at their demands. I replied that they certainly had the means and wherewithal to cover for Gregg, so the onus of covering up his extracurricular activities shouldn't fall on me.

The man sitting next to Spence then uttered a question that I will never forget: "I can withstand a background investigation … can you?" I responded, "Yes … I can withstand a background investigation." My response essentially concluded the 20-minute meeting. Spence was quite irate with me when I refused to write their letter, and he berated me as he showed me to the door. Unbeknownst to me, I would never see Spence again.

I've since confirmed that Spence's friend was indeed in Bush's cabinet. He was obviously attempting to aid and abet Spence's cover up of Gregg's extracurricular activities, even though Spence was freefalling in crack addiction. I have great difficulties believing that a man of immense power would put his cabinet position, career, and family on the line to help a degenerate crack addict even if they were friends and the latter once provided him with adolescent boys. It only makes sense if the cabinet member was in the same shadowy network as Spence or if that shadowy network had compromised him.

•••

A few days after my meeting with Spence and his "friend," I flew to Bolivar, Tennessee, to attend an air-training seminar at the Bolivar Aviation School. On February 29th, a few days after my arrival in Tennessee, I received a frantic phone call from Jimmy. He blurted out that the Secret Service had smashed down the door of the house on 34th Place, and the agents had held him at gunpoint as they ravaged the premises. Jimmy said the agents arrested him for possession of narcotics, and he had spent the night in jail. Over the years, I've found flying to be a serene, meditative experience, but I flew back to Maryland the next day in a frenzied state, and then I drove into D.C. The Secret Service had sealed the house on 34th Place and also my apartment on New Hampshire. As I drove by both locations, I came to the painful realization that I couldn't withstand a background check.

I concluded that I needed to find a place to sleep, and, needless to say, I didn't think phoning Aunt Josephine would be prudent. I ultimately contacted Richard Rausch, who was the doorkeeper for the House of Representatives. Richard was a client who had grown to be a close friend. Richard told me that he had heard about the raid, and he unhesitantly offered to accommodate me. He had a two-bedroom apartment on 2nd Street Southeast that was around the corner from the Library of Congress.

As I drove to Richard's apartment, I pondered the possible scope of my troubles, and I felt considerable ambivalence about my predicament. The Secret Service had conducted the raids, so a part of me thought that I had incurred the wrath of the federal government. But conversely, I also thought that the feds would be unlocking a Pandora's Box if they indicted me due to my first-hand knowledge of Spence's illicit activities, which included the malfeasance of the Secret Service, high-ranking military personnel, congressmen, and at least one member of the presidential cabinet. And, of course, blackmail and the interstate trafficking of children.

Richard greeted me at the door of his apartment with a cheerful hug. He was a tall, thin 53-year-old who appeared much older due to years of chain smoking and his unadulterated love of Jack Daniels. Although Richard's speech and mannerisms were very polished and refined, his lifestyle had carved premature furrows on his face.

Stepping into Richard's apartment was like entering a time warp to the 1960s. The living room was sparsely furnished with an orange couch and an orange chair. Various trinkets from the Kennedy administration were tacked up on the light green walls of his living room. Books were stacked up towards the ceiling, and magazines dating back to the early 1960s overflowed the living room into the hallway. Although Richard's apartment smelled like an ashtray, I was very grateful to him for providing me with a sanctuary.

Richard had an insuppressible élan that made me feel I would prevail through my current dilemma, and he also possessed a great sense of humor. He often alluded to his mother's vast fortune, and he frequently referred to being transported to a seemingly carefree nirvana "… when mother dies." Richard was originally from Iowa, and I never knew whether or not his mother had a vast fortune, but "when mother dies" was a recurrent punch line to his witticisms and amusing anecdotes.

Shortly after I arrived at Richard's, both the *Washington Post* and the *Washington Times* phoned me, but I shunned their requests for interviews. I was slightly surprised that neither state nor federal law enforcement contacted me in the wake of the raids, which reinforced my belief that the government was too apprehensive to prosecute me due to the illicit malfeasance I had witnessed over the years. When the government didn't show an inclination to indict me, I continued running my escort service—albeit at a greatly reduced volume. I scaled back my business by 75 percent. Travis was game to resume answering the phones, so I rented an apartment for him that was near DuPont Circle.

I had been at Richard's for three months, and I hadn't heard a word from the feds. After they lulled me into a false sense of security, I contacted the Secret Service, requesting that it unseal the house and apartment, and also return the items that it had impounded. The Secret Service, however, was inflexible and refused to unseal the house and apartment or return any of my possessions. Indeed, the Secret Service wasn't even willing to return the presidential cufflinks that Paul Balach had given me.

I was in the midst of the calm before the storm.

In June, the U.S. Attorney for the District of D.C., Jay Stephens, impaneled a grand jury to investigate my escort service and me. Stephens told the media that the crux of the investigation involved prostitution and credit card fraud. When I read that the investigation would focus on credit card fraud, I had the disconcerting answer to a lingering question that had truly baffled me: Tony's request that I process credit cards.

In 1989, the Secret Service was an arm of the Department of the Treasury, and it was tasked with investigating credit card fraud. After the U.S. Attorney announced that the grand jury would be largely investigating credit card fraud, I was suddenly stricken with the epiphany that Tony had led me down the primrose path of processing credit cards, so the Secret Service could control its investigation of me when it decided the time was ripe to take me down. The media reported I used umbrella organizations in Florida, West Virginia, and the D.C. area to process credit cards. I later learned that the credit card processing service in Miami, Florida was a front for a Secret Service sting.

I'm fully cognizant of the fact that I can't prove Tony's existence, because he was essentially a phantom, or, perhaps, I should say, a spook. He wafted in and out of my life, and he was circumspect about not leaving his existential fingerprints. But without Tony's intrusion, it doesn't make sense that I would use a credit card processing service in Miami, Florida, that was a Secret Service front, because Robert was thoroughly willing to process credit cards for the 20 percent cut he received from their proceeds.

•••

Shortly after the grand jury was impaneled, the feds initiated their reign of terror against my family, friends, and the patrons of my escort service, but, surprisingly, they largely left me alone. The Secret Service executed search warrants on my mother and sister. My mother and sister were living in Williamson when a Secret Service motorcade slowly and conspicuously rolled through the streets of Williamson. Secret Service agents wielding machine guns smashed through the front door of mother's house and spent two hours ransacking her home.

After Secret Service agents besieged my mother, they then besieged my sister and her husband with the same modus operandi. They smashed through the front door of their home, and, holding my brother-in-law at gunpoint, they ransacked their house. I had stashed a Macintosh, which stored all of my records, at my sister's. When the Secret Service found the computer, my sister told me that one agent exclaimed: "We hit the mother lode!"

The *Washington Times* reported on the campaign of terror and intimidation Secret Service agents unleashed on my mother and sister. But the Secret Service's campaign of terror against my family didn't conclude after its agents executed their search warrants. Secret Service agents made repeated visitations to my mother and sister after the initial raids on their homes.

My mother decided to flee the mounting pressure, and she visited her siblings in San Antonio, Texas. By 1989, Aunt Emma Jean and Uncle Harold had joined Uncle Clarence in San Antonio, and my mother sought refuge with Aunt Emma Jean. Secret Service agents actually followed my mother to San Antonio and conspicuously parked across the street from Emma Jean's house throughout my mother's visit.

My mother's plight was truly heartbreaking for me. Throughout the years, as I sat at my desk answering the phones every night, I regularly phoned my mother, and we talked for hours. My problematic exodus from Williamson and her reimmersion in religion had strained our relationship, but my near nightly calls to her had positively reshaped our relationship. I think that she was much more aghast at the fact that I was running a gay escort service than at her brutalization by the Secret Service's thuggery. Although my mother deeply loved me and accepted my heartfelt apologies, I felt acute anguish over her predicament.

The Secret Service also extended its reign of terror to the escorts I employed and to some of my patrons. During this period, a number of patrons phoned me and related tales of Secret Service intimidation. Secret Service agents had visited their homes and told their spouses that their husbands were patrons of my escort service. Patrons who had become personal friends, such as Alan Barron and Charles Dutcher, started distancing themselves from me.

I eventually found myself under surveillance by, presumably, the Secret Service. Black sedans with tinted windows parked across the street from Richard's apartment. They made absolutely no effort to conceal their surveillance, and it was woefully obvious to Richard too. But he was undaunted. "When mother dies" he said, "we'll be able to disappear without a trace."

In addition to unleashing a reign of terror, the government started spinning a propaganda campaign to cover up the factual realities of my case. The U.S. Attorney for the District of Columbia told the media that Washington D.C.'s Metro Police learned of my escort service, because a "local hotel" complained about suspected prostitution activities, and the Secret Service only became involved in the case to assist D.C.'s Metro Police Department in its investigation of credit card fraud. If the Secret Service was mobilized only after the Metro Police requested that it assist with a credit card fraud case, I find it rather mystifying that the Secret Service ultimately spearheaded the investigation.

Since the February raid, I had shunned repeated attempts by the media to interview me, but the government's reign of terror against my family and friends made me increasingly livid. So I finally dispensed a few choice quotes to the *Washington Times*. "Somebody set us up because they were scared about what we knew about high government officials. I think it's because they wanted to get our files. We had some very big-name clients in all walks of life—on Capitol Hill, the military, and even the White House. You'd be surprise.... And anyways, if they do try to indict me, I'll have some good stories to tell."

I initially thought that I was immune to prosecution due to the mind-boggling malfeasance and illicit activity I had personally witnessed. But after I parceled out those quotes to the *Washington Times,* I came to the unsettling conclusion that murdering me would save the government from a scandal of epic proportions.

William J. Casey

CHAPTER ELEVEN

A LIGHT IN THE SHADOWS

As I retreated from the maddening crowd at Richard's apartment, I felt that the truth would eventually emerge about the sub rosa universe of blackmail and power politics that had swallowed me, even though I wasn't quite sure if the truth would set me free or result in my premature demise. The government, or perhaps a very corrupt subgenus of the government, unquestionably had a vested interest in obscuring the truth. But the enterprise of Spence et al. was so vast that I thought it would be nearly impossible to cover up.

For example, the pedophile network operated by Spence and King was transcontinental in scope. Child welfare personnel in Nebraska attempted to expose the network, but their pleas were simply ignored by state law enforcement. A Nebraska senate subcommittee ultimately investigated King's interstate exploitation of children. A rash of mysterious deaths, including the enigmatic death of the subcommittee's investigator, followed in the wake of senators' efforts, and both federal and state authorities would declare that King wasn't involved in the abuse or pandering of a single child.

At the end of June, the truth indeed started leaking out via the *Washington Times,* which initially struck me as an unlikely wellspring for the truth, because of the newspaper's archconservative bent, and its partisan support for the Bush administration. The *Washington Times* managed to obtain a cache of credit card vouchers that had been processed by Robert through Professional Services, and the credit card vouchers presented its reporters with a constellation of names. Various clients phoned me, and much to their chagrin relayed that *Washington Times* reporters had recently contacted them.

On June 29th, the *Washington Times* published a front-page article that focused on my escort service and also on Spence's shenanigans. The banner headline read: "Homosexual Prostitution Inquiry Ensnares VIPs with Reagan, Bush." And the headline was followed by a subheadline: "Callboys Took Midnight Tour of the White House."

The article's first sentence read: "A homosexual prostitution ring is under investigation by federal and District authorities and includes among its clients key officials of the Reagan and Bush administrations, military officers, congressional aides and U.S. and foreign businessmen with close ties to Washington's political elite..." The article's second paragraph discussed one of Spence's "middle-of-the-night" tours of the White House. Although the article didn't directly name Spence, it remarked that the tour's host was a "high-profile client" of my escort service.

The *Washington Times* was certainly diverging from the government's spin, because its reportage significantly deviated from the U.S. Attorney for D.C.'s stock response that the grand jury he impaneled in June to investigate me was primarily focusing credit card fraud and prostitution. In fact, the *Washington Times* article even mentioned that the U.S. Attorney for D.C., Jay Stephens, had a potential "conflict of interest" in his investigation of me due to the fact that he was the former deputy White House counsel to President Reagan, and the names of several of his "White House colleagues" were on the credit card vouchers. The article also noted that the U.S. Attorney's office stated that it would no longer cooperate with the *Washington Times* inquiry, even though it had initially consented to cooperate with the newspaper's investigation.

Unfortunately, the article outed Paul Balach and Charles Dutcher as homosexuals, which I thought was completely unnecessary. Paul immediately tendered his resignation as the Secretary of Labor's political personnel liaison to the White House. We had lunch a few weeks after the article was published, and I felt terrible for him. He was absolutely devastated. Paul's eyes welled with tears as he told me that he had been given the option of resigning or being fired. Paul's career never recovered, and he eventually committed suicide.

The next day, June 30th, the *Washington Times* launched a story about Spence's blackmail enterprise that was complimented by a banner headline: "Power Broker Served Drugs, Sex At Parties Bugged For Blackmail." The article's first sentence certainly summed up some of my experiences with Spence: "Craig J. Spence, an enigmatic figure who threw glittery parties for key officials of the Reagan and Bush administrations, media stars and top military officers, bugged the gatherings to compromise guests and spent up to $20,000 a month on male prostitutes, according to friends, acquaintances and records."

The article quoted various sources who were cognizant of Spence's Kalorama home being wired for clandestine surveillance. Three of the people in the know included a "former bodyguard," a former "Reagan administration official," and a "friend" of Spence's who discussed Spence "spying on guests" through the eight-foot two-way mirror in his living room. The article quoted a fourth individual, a "business associate" of Spence's, who said of Spence: "He was taping and blackmailing people."

The article also commented on a discussion between two friends of Spence's—CBS correspondent Liz Trotta and a Georgetown University law professor—who attended a party at his Kalorama home. The article said that they expressed their concerns to each other regarding Spence's deteriorating physical condition and behavior. And later in the evening, Spence told them that he had been listening to their conversation, and he didn't appreciate them talking behind his back.

After the article illuminated Spence's bugged home and his penchant for blackmail, it discussed his predilection for cocaine, noting that one of Spence's friends described him as an unabashed "coke freak." The article then discussed the blizzards of cocaine that Spence used to regale his partygoers. The *Washington Times* heard conflicting accounts about the genesis of Spence's cocaine connection. The newspaper reported that "several friends" said Spence boasted that U.S. military personnel smuggled the cocaine into the country from El Salvador, and other friends said that Spence acquired his stash of coke from "midlevel dealers" in D.C.

The *Washington Times* article outed Spence as the puppeteer behind the late night tour of the White House too: "One man who was on the tour but asked not to be named for fear it would damage his business said it was cleared by a uniformed Secret Service guard whom the man had seen attending Mr. Spence's parties as a bodyguard." And the newspaper would later report on additional late night White House tours that were choreographed by Spence.

Finally, the article alluded to Spence's CIA connections, noting a "businessman" who dealt with Spence told reporters that Spence often bragged that he worked for the CIA. Spence would tell *Washington Times* reporters that the CIA employed him, and the newspaper would eventually have intelligence sources confirm that Spence was indeed a CIA asset. Moreover, Spence later told the *Washington Times* that "friendly" intelligence agents had installed the blackmail equipment in his home.

The *Washington Times* articles on Spence validated that he spent up to $20,000 a month for escorts, his home was wired for blackmail, Secret Service agents moonlighted as his bodyguards, and at least one Secret Service agent gave Spence late night access to the White House with an escort in tow. The newspaper confirmed many of the events that I had witnessed firsthand.

The *Washington Times* eventually named a number of the powerbrokers who attended Spence's Kalorama soirées. His guests were a veritable who's who from the media and politics. Media pundits such as Eric Sevareid, Ted Koppel, and William Safire were in attendance at Spence's parties. High-flying politicians—including Senators John Glenn of Ohio and Frank Murkowski of Alaska—attended his get-togethers too. Spence's home was also a lure for various Republican movers and shakers, attracting former ambassadors Robert Neumann, Elliott Richardson, and James Lilly. Then-CIA Director William Casey and John Mitchell, the disgraced former attorney general under Richard Nixon, were personal friends of Spence who frequented his *soirées.*

Although Spence's home was a magnet for D.C. elites, I don't necessarily think that everyone who graced his parties was compromised. But on the other hand, many of Spence's partygoers were lubricated on alcohol before they had illicit drugs and a wide variety of sexual playmates, including children, dangled in front of them. If his partygoers succumbed to their temptations, they were undoubtedly compromised. An individual merely discussing illegal activities in Spence's home—like me—had the potential to be compromised.

As the *Washington Times* bore deeper and deeper into the enigma of Spence, I was astonished to read about the eddies of his sordid life in black and white—on the front-page of a newspaper. The levy of lies that had suppressed the truth about Spence for years was starting crumble, and I pondered its implications for me. I felt that it would be difficult for the government to cover up Spence's illicit activities now that the toothpaste was out of the tube. I also had a tendency to think that the government wouldn't take a chance on indicting me, because a trial would only publicize Spence's complicity with high-ranking federal officials and his connections to the Secret Service and perhaps even the CIA. But I wasn't quite sure if the *Washington Times'* articles about Spence enhanced my safety or endangered me.

I felt a potential risk to my life was CIA Director William Casey's patronage of my escort service. The *Washington Times* reported that William Casey attended parties at Spence's house, and Casey and Spence were "friends," but its reporters weren't aware that their friendship had a common denominator that entailed procuring gay escorts from me. William Casey started to phone me for gay escorts in 1986. Like Barney Frank, his preferred escort was an eighteen-year-old with minimal body hair and a slender swimmer's physique. Although he requested that I provide him with underage escorts, I told him that I wouldn't acquiesce to that request.

Casey met with the escorts at the Ritz-Carleton Hotel, when it was near DuPont Circle. After he was nude and splayed on a bed, he had the escorts rub oil over his body as he kissed and fondled them. Casey was old and withered, and the escorts didn't particularly savor their encounters with him. Casey came to my attention, because he wasn't able to have an erection, and the escorts that I employed were perplexed by both his elaborate rituals with the oil and his erectile dysfunction.

Casey died of cancer in May of 1987, so, when the *Washington Times* started to break stories about Spence and my escort service, Casey had drifted to the hereafter. Nevertheless, I was worried that his CIA cronies would want to bury his secret dalliances with young men—even if that involved burying me.

•••

I believe that the government responded to the *Washington Times* articles about Spence with a propaganda counter-offensive mounted by the *Washington Post*. The *Washington Post's* first assault on the *Washington Times* was a protracted article, "The Shadow World of Craig Spence," published in the middle of July, and it was a concerted effort to dismantle the *Washington Times* reportage on Spence. The article mocked the earlier headline floated by the *Washington Times*—"Power Broker Served Drugs, Sex at Parties Bugged for Blackmail"—by providing the veritable, unadulterated truth about Spence's get-togethers: "People sat around in a perimeter after dinner discussing trade policy, where American policy makers were ushered into circles of foreign visitors to make serious talk; parties to which Koppel would sometimes send a stand-in; parties so dull that even *Dossier* magazine wouldn't run the photographs."

The *Washington Post* even recycled quotes from a profile of Spence it had published in 1980: "Not since Ethel Kennedy used to give her famous Hickory Hill seminars for great minds of our times during the days of Camelot has anyone staged seminars successfully on a continuing social basis in Washington."

I don't doubt that Spence hosted drab cocktail parties and seminars, but he also hosted no holds barred orgies. The *Post* neglected to mention that the *Washington Times* collected irrefutable proof in the form of credit card vouchers that Spence spent up to $20,000 a month on escorts from my escort service. I seriously doubt that Ethel Kennedy spent up to $20,000 a month on male prostitutes.

The *Post's* "The Shadow World of Craig Spence" also dismantled the idea that Spence's house was bugged for blackmail, but its hatchet job was transparently disingenuous. The *Post* deployed a contrivance it coined the "skeptical guest" to debunk the notion that Spence's home had clandestine surveillance. The *Post's* "skeptical guest" was an unnamed source, and the *Post* even neglected to mention the source's gender or his or her relationship to Spence.

According to the *Post*, the "skeptical guest" was in attendance at a party in Spence's Kalorama home when a friend of Spence's, CBS correspondent Liz Trotta, "got down on her hands and knees in the living room and found wires and cables all over the room at floor level. She also found metal fasteners that could have been listening devices, she says, clipped to the bottom of a coffee table. A skeptical guest who witnessed this—who was familiar with the architecture and furnishings—said that one of the so-called bugs was a button-release on the table and that to his knowledge, there were no bugs."

Given the onslaught of erroneous press I've received over the years, I'm reluctant to ascribe inordinate intelligence to many in the media, but common sense would dictate that a veteran CBS correspondent could distinguish a bug from a "button-release" on a table. But, perhaps, because of the skeptical guest's expertise on "architecture and furnishings," he or she was able to provide the *Post* with the definitive truth?

I've previously mentioned a *Washington Times* article that discussed former CBS correspondent Liz Trotta and a Georgetown University law professor Richard Gordon discussing Spence's fading health during a party at his home, and Spence later expressing his umbrage to them for nattering behind his back. The *Post's* "skeptical guest" just happened to attend that party too.

And once more, the *Post* relayed the unequivocal truth from the perspective of the skeptical guest: "Spence confronted them later that night. 'I heard every word you said,' Gordon recalls Spence saying. 'You're conspiring against me. I've got this corner bugged.' And then he pointed to the ceiling. 'There was never a bug hanging over Professor Gordon's head,' says the same skeptical guest, who was also at that party. Another person there says that it was so obvious that Gordon and Trotta were gossiping about Spence all night he would not have needed bugs to guess what they were saying." (I have to agree with the "skeptical guest" on at least one point: the "bug" probably wasn't "hanging" over Trotta and Gordon's heads. It was most likely embedded in a light fixture or the crown molding.)

After the *Post* deployed the skeptical guest and "another person" to debunk the fact that Spence's house was bugged for blackmail, it descended into a rather absurd commentary: "Some believe that Spence may have been up to something with the electronic equipment that friends observed in the house. But Spence's clairvoyance, it seems, was strongest when his bodyguards were present and within earshot of the supposedly bugged conversations."

So now the *Post* acknowledged that Spence had "electronic equipment" in his home, even though in the preceding paragraph it had asserted that the bug uncovered by Trotta was, in actuality, a button-release on a table. The *Post* wanted to have its cake and eat it too by conceding that Spence had electronic equipment in his home, but ridiculing the fact that his home was bugged.

And the *Post's* remark about Spence's "clairvoyance" being heightened when his bodyguards were within "earshot" was rather disingenuous too. The *Post* doesn't question why Spence had a need for bodyguards. But in all likelihood, Spence needed constant protection, because he was the point man for blackmailing some of the most powerful men in the country—powerful men who almost certainly had access to their own thugs. Given Spence's penchant for blackmailing the powerful, I think his longevity had the potential to be violently curtailed if his private Praetorian Guard didn't vigilantly safeguard him.

Later in the article, the *Post* described Spence's bodyguards as "clean-cut college guys who also tended bar, parked cars and drove Spence around. Spence later started hiring Army men and Marines, especially large, well-built ones." I'm aware of Spence collecting bodyguards from the military, but the article made no mention of Spence's bodyguards being pulled from the ranks of the Secret Service, even though the *Washington Times* had been meticulous about nailing down that Spence had Secret Service agents moonlighting as his bodyguards.

The *Post's* "The Shadow World of Craig Spence" portrayed him as a high society bottom feeder who was more of a name-dropper than a powerbroker with high powered connections, and the article also attempted to dispel the notion that he was affiliated with the CIA. The article caricaturized Spence by having his friends discuss his rants of self-importance and name-dropping, which wouldn't be too difficult. After the *Post* made Spence appear as a mere cartoon character it dropped in the following paragraph: "Like the tales of espionage, the allegations about bugging were a regular subject of discussion among his friends. And again, they got their information from him [Spence]."

•••

A week after the *Washington Post* demolished the *Washington Times'* reportage on Spence's illicit activities, I found myself in the *Post's* character assassination crosshairs. Earlier in July, in the wake of the initial *Washington Times* articles, I granted the *Post* an interview, because I sincerely thought it was taking the torch from the *Washington Times* and following a parallel avenue of inquiry. But the *Post's* article on me, "From Small-Roots, a Big City Scandal," expended considerable ink dismantling my credibility, and it was also riddled with falsehoods.

The article's second paragraph dredged up the fallacious cover story about my exodus from Williamson. "First the 25-year-old funeral director was charged with making harassing phone calls to a competing funeral home. Later the state claimed he was overcharging on pauper funerals. Then there was the small matter of the exhumed coal miner's remains he didn't rebury for 42 days. He finally left town."

And, unfortunately, that was only the *Post's* initial character assassination salvo. The *Post* reported that the Mingo County prosecutor had given me the option of being charged with "misappropriating state funds" or resign as the Mingo County Medical Examiner, which is an absolute falsehood. I opted to resign as the Mingo County Medical Examiner, because I faced the specious misdemeanor of making harassing phone calls to the Ball Funeral Home, which I've previously explained. The *Post* then reported that I said I left Williamson on the day I resigned as Mingo County Medical Examiner—yet another falsehood. I continued to run the Vinson Funeral Home after I resigned as the Medical Examiner.

The *Post* also inserted bald-faced lies when it discussed my introduction into the escort business. The article reported that my entrée was answering an escort ad in the *Washington Blade* for Don's Capitol Escorts! The *Post* reportedly interviewed Donald Schey, who was the proprietor of Don's Capitol Escorts, and Schey reportedly said that I was one of his "busiest escorts." I find this account mindboggling due to the fact that I've never even met Donald Schey. The *Post* then reported that in 1987 I took over answering "Schey's telephones for a fee." And then I made my leap to being the proprietor of an escort service later that year when I bought a "service" for "$2,000" from a man who was dying of AIDS. The only morsel of truth in the *Post's* account of me becoming a D.C. madam was that I bought an escort service from a man dying of AIDS.

The *Post* then injected a whopping lie when it purportedly quoted me: "'I've had sex before with people who came to put in the telephone, but that doesn't mean C&P [telephone company] is into prostitution—and they charge $45 for a 15-minute installation,' said Vinson." It's certainly not my intention to disparage telephone linemen, but I've never met a telephone lineman who's stirred my libido.

"From Small-Roots, a Big City Scandal" also commented on my near maniacal ambition as I plotted and schemed "toward a monopoly on Washington gay escort services." I admit that I infused my escort venture with an entrepreneurial innovation, but I definitely didn't conspire to cartelize D.C. prostitution as if I were the Richard III of gay escorts. In the paragraph where the

Post discusses my scheming to monopolize Washington's gay escort services, it said that I agreed to process credit cards for other services, including "Metro Date," which was a "service" I had previously attempted to purchase. Yet again the *Post's* reportage derailed itself from reality—I started Metro Date!

The article reported that I "bought an expensive new sports car and mailed $500 a month home" to my mother. The *Post's* latter comments are outright lies. I drove my 280Z to Washington, D.C., and I never sold it or traded it in for "an expensive new sports car." Moreover, I never sent my mother $500 a month. My mother's various business ventures and real estate holdings had made her a millionaire, so it just doesn't add up that I would send her $500 a month. I could cite additional lies in "From Small-Roots, a Big City Scandal," but I think it's evident that the *Post's* article on me was not fair and impartial, or, for that matter, even truthful.

•••

The *Washington Post's* denouement to stamp its imprimatur on the cover up of Spence's activities, "The Bombshell That Didn't Explode; Behind the Times' 'Scoop' and Press Coverage of the Call-Boy Ring," was published in early August. This article had the same cynical tone and tenor as the *Post's* previous articles, but now the newspaper conscripted the *Los Angeles Times* and *New York Times* to jump on its bandwagon. "We checked into it; we sent reporters out when they raided the house in February and again when they had the eviction," said the Washington bureau chief of the *Los Angeles Times*. "We never did turn up with anything that looked like a national story."

After the *Post* quoted the *Los Angeles Times* bureau chief, the *New York Times'* Washington bureau chief endorsed the *Post's* spin. "I don't take the *Washington Times* seriously as a journalistic entity, so I view with suspicion almost anything that they do," he said. "I don't deny a raid on this house and that there's obviously some kind of investigation going on. But so far I haven't seen any evidence that it means what they say it means."

In addition to the *New York Times* and *Los Angeles Times,* the *Washington Post* buttressed its propaganda campaign with sources that were delighted to reinforce its disinformation—government sources. The *Post* wrote of its first source: "... a key law enforcement official came to lunch at the *Post* and assured the staff that the investigation was primarily on credit card fraud." As I recall, several administration officials, including the U.S. attorney general, were telling the media that Watergate was much ado about nothing, so I find it perplexing that the *Post* was all ears about Spence's blackmail enterprise, but it was vehement when contesting the administration's official position about Watergate.

The *Post's* "The Bombshell That Didn't Explode" article weighed in on the newspaper's meticulous reporting on its Spence profile—"The Shadow World of Craig Spence." The *Post's* editor of the "Style section," where the Spence article was published, expressed his kudos for the story, saying that the *Post* "took the time to get [the story] done the way it ought to be done, and I'm very proud of the story—a very interesting, sophisticated, classic Style story on a very interesting Washington phenomenon." Perhaps the Style section was the right fit for the Spence article, because I'm not aware of the *Post* having a Powerbroker Blackmail section.

CHAPTER TWELVE

THE MIGHTY WURLIZTER

Tony vanished two or three months before the Secret Service raids, and Spence, too, would ultimately recede. But his vanishing act would culminate in a surreal sequence of events that was patently Craig Spence. After the federal grand jury investigating me served Spence with a subpoena, he scrambled to whereabouts unknown. While Spence was AWOL, various accounts had him surfacing in Florida, Boston, and New Hampshire. In July, Spence materialized in New York City with a near bang: the NYPD arrested him for possession of a handgun, cocaine, and a crack pipe.

Spence was ensconced at Manhattan's upscale Barbizon Hotel on the Upper East Side, smoking crack with a 22-year-old male prostitute, which was certainly a consistent pattern of behavior for him. Spence then placed a frantic 911 call. The NYPD officers who reportedly responded to the call bounced into Spence as he darted out of his hotel room. "This guy Craig Spence comes running out of the room screaming that the other guy has a gun," one of the responding NYPD officers told a reporter. "Spence claimed the kid had taken the gun and intimidated him and snatched $6,000 out of his hand."

The NYPD charged Spence with criminal possession of a pistol and possession of an illegal drug, and he was thrown in downtown Manhattan's "the Tombs," a vast jail that serves as a repository for those awaiting arraignment or trial. Three days after his arrest, Spence was released on his own recognizance, but he was staring at an eight-year sentence. I harken back to the *Washington Post* comparing Craig Spence and his seminars to Ethel Kennedy and her seminars, but I don't ever recall reading a newspaper account about Ethel Kennedy being arrested for possession of a handgun and crack cocaine.

In the wake of Spence's arrest in New York, a pair of *Washington Times* reporters scurried to New York City, and they eventually found Spence at a friend's posh East Side apartment. The reporters noted that the powerbroker had fallen on hard times: he wore a grubby white knit shirt, crumpled khakis, and ramshackle Reebok running shoes, and he was uncharacteristically unshaven.

Spence eventually gave the reporters a protracted interview that was bizarre even by Spence's standards, which were indeed bizarre. During the interview, Spence clenched a dispenser of double-edge razor blades. He ultimately dispensed one of the razor blades, and used it to caress his arms. Spence then shoved the razorblade toward the chests of the reporters. "I am not a person to fool with," he snapped. "You should know that by now."

When Spence finished threatening the reporters with the razorblade, he embarked on an extended soliloquy of self-importance that was quite familiar to me. He mentioned that he had performed a myriad of assignments for the CIA, and his assignments were critical to covert actions in Vietnam, Japan, Central America, and the Middle East. "How do you think a little faggot like me moved in the circles I did?" Spence asked. "It's because I had contacts at the highest levels of this government. They'll deny it, but how do they make me go away when so many of them have been at my house, at my parties, and at my side?" Spence wasn't enthusiastic about testifying before the grand jury that was investigating me. He told the reporters that he would "never be brought back alive" to testify before the grand jury.

Spence managed to live below the media's radar for a few months after his debacle in New York City. In October, however, he threw an extravagant birthday party for himself in D.C., and fortunately I wasn't invited. "The rumors of my death are greatly exaggerated," he said to his friends at the party. Shortly after his birthday party, Spence delivered a "video postcard" to various friends and associates.

In the video, Spence was seated on a leather chair in his dining room, and he waxed philosophic about the government, intelligence community, and life's changing fortunes. He also parceled out a parable about the intelligence fraternity: "Some of you may know when it comes to the intelligence community, there is no such thing as coincidence. Now, I'm not sure I've seen the whole picture yet myself." Spence eventually ended his "video postcard" with buoyant nationalism: "I'll close by telling you I'm sure that in the end the truth will come out, and this too will pass. Now, I may be naïve about my optimism, but I'm an American, proud of my country, and confident of the fairness of its people. So take heart, good friends, and share that pride and that confidence with me. Good night and God bless."

A few weeks later, Spence's lifeless body was found in a hotel room at Boston's Ritz-Carlton. He wore a black tuxedo, white shirt, bow tie, white suspenders, black socks, and shoes. Next to Spence's body was a newspaper clipping about then-CIA Director William Webster's attempts to protect CIA agents who were summoned to testify before government inquiries.

Spence also taped a suicide note on the room's mirror: "Chief, consider this my resignation, effective immediately. As you always said, you can't ask others to make a sacrifice if you are not ready to do the same. Life is duty. God bless America." The suicide note also had an uncharacteristically considerate afterthought: "To the Ritz, please forgive this inconvenience." I only wish Spence had been that polite when he inhabited the world of living. The letter taped to the mirror ended with a Japanese phrase: "Nisei Bei," which means second-generation American. So on the threshold of death, Spence finally confessed to his humble origins.

I would be remiss if I didn't mention that the U.S. attorney for D.C. took an inordinate interest in Spence's death. Although the Boston Medical Examiner's Office routinely released the cause of people's death within days of their passing, a top-ranking Boston city official said that the U.S. Attorney for D.C. requested that Spence's death certificate not be released. A second

Boston official commented about the U.S. attorney's inordinate interest in Spence's death.

But a spokesman for the U.S. Attorney was mum about the U.S. attorney's unorthodox demand: "The investigation is ongoing before the grand jury. I cannot make any comment about it." The Secret Service was the government entity that did the heavy lifting to cover up Spence's activities with regards to threats and intimidation, but, as I will later explain, the U.S. attorney for D.C. was the government entity that finessed the cover up.

The Internet is rife with speculation that Spence was murdered or "suicided," but I'm not of that belief. Spence was dying of AIDS, and it's evident to me that the shadowy network that had floated his ultra-posh lifestyle, and also his vast expenditures on escorts, drugs, and bodyguards had rescinded its finances, because he had become too dysfunctional. So suicide was essentially his only option.

•••

After my personal interactions with Spence, I came to the conclusion that his shadowy network was affiliated with the CIA, or perhaps a rogue element within the CIA. It was almost effortless for the *Washington Post* to annihilate Spence's credibility, because he had become an absolute lunatic in his final days. I'll be the first to admit that Spence was never the paragon of mental health, but before he plunged into crack addiction he had the potential to be remarkably cogent despite his seismic narcissism and amoral personality. Spence's cogency was evinced by the various feats he managed to accomplish, and his amoral personality was an occupational requisite for a blackmail artist who procured men, women, and even children for his blackmail targets.

The *Washington Post* focused on Spence's personal confessions, government disavowals, and such contrivances as the "skeptical guest" when debunking Spence's intelligence connections and his blackmail activities. The newspaper conveniently omitted or ignored the numerous sources that had been painstakingly amassed by the *Washington Times* concerning Spence's intelligence connections and his blackmail activities, and also the fact that the *Washington Times* had intelligence sources confirm that Spence was indeed a CIA asset. I also have a tendency to think that William Casey's involvement with both Spence and gay escorts is perhaps additional corroboration that Spence's blackmail activities were affiliated with the CIA.

I've had years, in and out of prison, to ponder the maelstrom of skullduggery and intrigue that overwhelmed me like a tsunami, and also the *Washington Post's* cover up of Spence's crimes. I'm not a "conspiracy theorist," but rather I'm someone whom the vagaries of fate placed near the epicenter of sprawling conspiracy. I think I've demonstrated that the *Washington Post* aided and abetted the government's cover up of Spence's enterprise, and over the years I've come across a very interesting relationship between the *Washington Post* and the CIA as I've attempted to understand the conspiracy that engulfed me.

Shortly after the CIA was formed in 1948, the agency initiated Operation Mockingbird, which was a campaign to influence popular perception through various front organizations and the media in the United States and abroad. Frank Wisner, head of the CIA's Office of Policy Coordination, oversaw Operation Mockingbird, and Wisner boasted that he was the maestro of a "mighty Wurlitzer" that was "capable of playing any propaganda tune he desired."

The Mighty Wurlitzer: How the CIA Played America, published by Harvard University Press, provides a sweeping overview of Operation Mockingbird. But a second book, *Katharine the Great,* written by former *Village Voice* journalist Deborah Davis, is a biographical sketch of *Washington Post* publisher Katharine Graham, and it focuses specifically on the clandestine connections between the CIA and *Washington Post.* According to *Katharine the Great* and numerous sources, the CIA's Frank Wisner tapped then-*Washington Post* publisher Philip Graham to be the CIA's Operation Mockingbird point man to infiltrate the media.

In *Katherine the Great,* Davis quoted a former CIA agent who discussed meetings between CIA personnel and Philip

Graham in which they conferred about the availability and prices of journalists: "You could get a journalist cheaper than a good call girl, for a couple hundred dollars a month." (I've often heard the comparison between journalists and prostitutes, but I think that comparison potentially denigrates the profession of prostitution. Most prostitutes aren't willing to destroy a life to turn a trick, but many journalists will handily destroy a life to land a story—even if the story is about trivial nonsense.)

"By the early 1950s," Davis wrote in *Katharine the Great*, "Wisner 'owned' respected members of the *New York Times, Newsweek,* CBS, and other communications vehicles, plus stringers, four to six hundred in all, according to a former CIA analyst." Davis also noted that Philip Graham stocked the *Washington Post* with writers and editors who had "intelligence backgrounds."

In addition to spotlighting the relationship between the CIA and Philip Graham, Davis examined the connections between the CIA and Ben Bradlee, the *Washington Post's* executive editor from 1968 to 1991. Bradlee was the executive editor of the *Post* during the newspaper's exposure of Watergate and also when it covered up Spence's network. Bradlee has been portrayed as the *Post's* salty editor who spurred on the "boys"—Woodward and Bernstein's—quest for truth as they toppled the Nixon administration. But Davis reported on a different side of former naval intelligence officer Ben Bradlee.

Bradlee was a descendant of Boston bluebloods, and he landed at the *Washington Post* as a young reporter in 1948. After three years at the *Post,* Davis reported that Graham pulled a few strings to help Bradlee become a press attaché stationed at the U.S. embassy in Paris. While in France, Bradlee developed a number of overt, yet interesting, ties to the CIA. He divorced his first wife and married Antoinette Pinchot, whose sister was married to CIA agent Cord Meyer. Davis asserts Meyer was a "principal operative" in Operation Mockingbird. Bradlee's new wife was also a close friend of the CIA's James Jesus Angleton who at the time was responsible for the collection of foreign intelligence in Europe. Angleton was later chief of the CIA's Counterintelligence for more than twenty years.

I've personally experienced guilt by association, and I've concluded that it's often an ill-fated formula for speculation. But in the first printing of *Katharine the Great*, Davis wrote that Bradlee "produced CIA material" when he was a press attaché in Paris. According to Davis, Bradlee churned out CIA propaganda regarding the Rosenbergs' case as a response to the French newspaper, *Le Monde*, which ran a story declaring that the U.S. had framed Ethel and Julius Rosenberg, who were the couple accused of imparting A-bomb secrets to the Soviets and sentenced to death. The *Le Monde* article outraged the CIA chief in Paris, because the agency was having difficulties selling the Cold War to a European public who feared that the McCarthy witch-hunts were ushering in a new wave of fascism.

After Bradlee read *Katharine the Great*, he quickly dispatched a threatening letter to Davis' publisher Harcourt Brace Jovanovich, one of the largest book publishers in the world. Bradlee's letter made some very unbecoming statements about Davis: "Miss Davis is lying ... I never produced CIA material ... what I can do is to brand Miss Davis as a fool and to put your company in that special little group of publishers who don't give a shit for the truth."

William Jovanovich, president and CEO of Harcourt Brace Jovanovich, apparently didn't want to be branded in that "little group of publishers who don't give a shit for the truth" by one of the most powerful newspapers in the country, so he ordered 20,000 copies of *Katharine the Great* to be destroycd, even though the Harcourt Brace Jovanovich catalog announced that *Katharine the Great* would be their top non-fiction selection and the publisher even nominated the book for an American Book Award. After Jovanovich turned 20,000 of *Katharine the Great* into pulp, he received a letter from Katharine the Great: "The whole theme of the book is so fanciful," wrote Katharine Graham, "that it defies serious discussion: that Ben, Phil (her deceased husband), and others worked for the CIA ..."

Davis sued Harcourt Brace for breach of contract. The case was eventually settled, and the rights for the book reverted back to Davis, but she couldn't find a major publisher who had the nerve to flirt with *Katharine the Great*. Finally, about seven years later, a small publisher in D.C. republished the book. In the interim, Davis sent several Freedom of Information Act requests to the government and landed some interesting documentation from the State Department about the fact that Bradlee "produced CIA material."

The State Department documents uncovered by Davis stated that three days after the *Le Monde* article appeared, the Paris CIA chief dispatched Bradlee to New York to collect documentation from the federal prosecutors on the Rosenberg case, so the CIA could mount a counter-offensive in the European press. Bradlee ultimately wrote a 30,000-word rundown and analysis of the government's case against the Rosenbergs with the CIA's topspin.

After Bradlee's tenure as a press attaché, he became a Paris-based foreign correspondent for *Newsweek*. I've already mentioned Davis reporting that the CIA's Wisner said he "owned" several media outlets, including *Newsweek*. In 1957, Bradlee returned to the United States, and he continued to write for *Newsweek* as a Washington bureau correspondent.

Bradlee's career at *Newsweek* took an upward but enigmatic twist in 1961. The cover story purports that *Newsweek* was up for sale, and Bradlee made a late night phone call to a man he barely knew—Philip Graham—and inquired if Graham wanted to purchase *Newsweek*. It just so happened that Graham thought it was an outstanding idea, and seventeen days later he shelled out $15 million to acquire *Newsweek*. He then made Bradlee *Newsweek's* Washington bureau chief. After Graham's suicide in 1963, Graham's widow eventually bestowed the title of managing editor of the *Washington Post* on Bradlee in 1965. (Interestingly, Frank Wisner committed suicide two years after Philip Graham.)

Rolling Stone published a 1977 article about the CIA's infiltration of the media that was penned by Carl Bernstein. The Bernstein article was published in the wake of the U.S. Senate's

Church Committee hearings that investigated a plethora of domestic and foreign crimes committed by the CIA. Although Bernstein wrote his *Rolling Stone* article under the auspices of uncovering the Church Committee's cover up between the CIA and media, I believe it's within the realm of reason that Bernstein's article covered up the *Washington Post's* links to the CIA. Bernstein's *Rolling Stone* article made no mention of Bradlee's ties to the CIA, and, in fact, almost exonerates the *Washington Post* staff of any ties to the CIA: "All editors-in-chief and managing editors of the *Post* since 1950 say they knew of no formal Agency relationship with either stringers or members of the *Post* staff. 'If anything was done it was done by Phil without our knowledge,' said one. Agency officials, meanwhile, make no claim that *Post* staff members have had covert affiliations with the Agency while working for the paper."

Given Philip Graham's zealous overtures to ingratiate the CIA with numerous media corporations and publications, and his padding the ranks of the *Washington Post* with former intelligence officers, I feel it broaches absurd to think that he didn't avail the *Washington Post* to the CIA's endeavors.

Ironically, if it were not for the conservative *Washington Times* with its neo-religious, anti-homosexual slant, I would have zero corroboration about the blackmail enterprise of Spence et al. I forgot to mention that the Reverend Sun Myung Moon owned the *Washington Times,* and I think it's a rather sad commentary on the American media when a Moonie-owned media outlet is the only news source providing Americans with the truth about a blackmail enterprise that's subverting their political system.

Greta Van Susteren

CHAPTER THIRTEEN

SLEEPLESS NIGHTS

Meanwhile, as I was ensconced at Richard's apartment, the grand jury that was "investigating" me wended through the summer, winter, and into the spring of 1990. I became exceedingly perplexed by the duration of the grand jury. Although most of my friends weren't called to testify, Secret Service agents nonetheless harassed them, and I subsequently found myself being ostracized by most of the people in my social network. My mother and sister were also sent letters that threatened to indict them. I ultimately came to the conclusion that the authorities overseeing my case were scheming to isolate me, and the government's tactics of uncertainty and intimidation were taking a toll on my emotional wellbeing. I started to suffer from insomnia, and I eventually acquired a prescription for Xanax to help me sleep.

As I would learn, the grand jury process has the potential to be seriously flawed, even though the phrase "grand jury" has authoritative connotations—like the gods on Mount Olympus have sent down a decree. A grand jury makes the initial decision to indict (formally accuse) a criminal defendant to stand trial. But unlike a standard trial, a grand jury proceeding is cloaked in secrecy: Grand juries aren't open to the public, and the identity of the witnesses who testify and the content of their testimony are never disclosed. Moreover, there is no cross-examination or presentation of the defense's case. The special prosecutor of a grand jury calls the witnesses, questions the witnesses, and selects the evidence that is shown to the grand jurors, and grand jurors are normal, everyday citizens who have shown up for jury duty and have been funneled to a grand jury.

Generally, only witnesses and evidence deemed relevant by special prosecutors are presented, and special prosecutors are in a unique position to influence grand jurors' judgments in a particular direction. Commenting about the powers of persuasion a special prosecutor has over grand jurors, a former chief appellate judge of New York state once famously remarked that a special prosecutor could persuade grand jurors to "indict a ham sandwich."

Jay Stephens, the U.S. Attorney for D.C., appointed Alan Strasser, the Assistant U.S. Attorney for D.C. and chief of the felony trial division, to be the special prosecutor of the grand jury investigating me. Strasser received his bachelor's degree in economics from Yale University in 1974, and he was a 1977 graduate of Harvard Law School. He joined the office of U.S. Attorney for D.C. in 1980.

Despite Strasser's lofty academic credentials, the grand jury he directed served a ham and swiss on rye to the public. He never called Robert, Jimmy, Travis, or me to testify before the grand jury that was ostensibly investigating our operation of an escort service. At the time, I thought it was rather odd. I'm also not aware of Strasser calling the escorts I employed to testify. Unfortunately, my mother was subpoenaed to testify before the grand jury. Although I processed a modest number of credit cards through her ambulance service, she had zero knowledge about the operations of my escort service.

The ever-dogged reporters of the *Washington Times* questioned many of Spence's partygoers and other individuals who were enmeshed with Spence. The reporters even managed to ferret out witnesses who had been called before the grand jury, and some of them broke their vows of secrecy on the condition that the *Washington Times* grant them anonymity.

A *Washington Times* article, commenting on the grand jury's intrigues, confirmed my lingering suspicion that the grand jury proceeding was a ham and swiss on rye. The article revealed that the newspaper's reporters had contacted "a number of principal witnesses and active participants in the case" and "discovered that few of them had been interviewed, and only a handful had been asked to testify before the grand jury." The article also noted that Robert, Jimmy, Travis and I hadn't been called to testify, nor had the "high-profile friends of Mr. Spence's who attended parties at his Kalorama home ..."

Washington Times reporters interviewed "a longtime acquaintance of Mr. Spence's" who had been called before the grand jury. The article mentioned that he "had spent considerable time as a guest in his [Spence's] home," and he was "a participant in one of the late-night White House tours." The *Washington Times* reported that the "witness was not asked any questions about credit cards, Mr. Spence's alleged involvement with the homosexual call-boy ring or about the ring itself." The witness told the reporters that one of the grand jury's primary concerns was establishing if Spence had been in the possession of purloined White House china that dated back to the Truman administration.

Spence was involved in pandering children, pandering adults, blackmailing powerbrokers, procuring illicit drugs, etc., so I find it mindboggling that one of the grand jury's primary concerns was whether or not he had absconded with some of the White House's Truman china. The *Washington Times* even commented about the grand jury being askew: "The grand jury investigation begun in June by U.S. Attorney Jay Stephens was described as a 'credit card' probe. It is not clear, however, how vigorous federal prosecutors have been nor where the case may be headed." The *Washington Times* article that questioned the vigor of federal prosecutors in the grand jury proceedings sought answers from Jay Stephens and Alan Strasser, but its reporters hit a firewall when both refused to comment.

•••

When I regrettably granted an interview to the *Washington Post* in early July of 1989, shortly after the grand jury was impaneled, one of its reporters requested to interview my mother, and my mother consented. Afterward, she phoned me and suggested that I meet with a Washington, D.C.-based attorney, whom the

Washington Post reporter had recommended. The attorney recommended by the *Washington Post* reporter just happened to be Greta Van Susteren.

I phoned Van Susteren shortly after my mother suggested that I contact her, and we set up an appointment for the following week. In July of 1989, Van Susteren's office was located on 22nd Street Northwest near DuPont Circle. Ironically, her office was about a block from Shooters. Driving to her office the morning of our initial meeting, I distinctly remember the radiant sun, azure sky, and gentle breeze. Despite the near perfect weather, I felt suffocated by anxiety and worries as I watched the denizens of D.C. absorbing the pristine morning. I longed for a life that allowed me to appreciate a beautiful day, and I hoped Van Susteren would enable me to restore my life to normalcy.

Van Susteren's office was housed on the second floor of a three-story brownstone. A receptionist greeted me as I walked in, and she directed me to a sofa. The reception area had hardwood floors, beige walls, and an austere decorum. When I sat on the sofa, I glanced at an adjacent end table that was arrayed with magazines. As I contemplated paging through a magazine, Van Susteren strolled into the reception area and amicably introduced herself. She was short, casually dressed in blue jeans, and she had a thick mane of blond hair. Shortly after we made eye contact, I noticed her asymmetrical smile. We exchanged a brief introduction, and I followed Van Susteren into her office.

After I sat down in a well-cushioned chair in front of Van Susteren's desk, she seated herself behind her desk. Her office had the same austere decorum as the reception room. The beige walls displayed her various degrees, and I noticed three or four cardboard boxes, filled with files, resting on the floor next to her desk. She came across as very sharp and articulate, and I was quite impressed. She gave me an overview of her education and some of her prior cases. Van Susteren discussed her judicial pedigree—her father had been a judge. But she neglected to tell me that her father was also the best friend of crazy Joe McCarthy and his campaign manager for the U.S. Senate. As she spoke, I was transfixed by the asymmetry of her mouth.

Our initial meeting lasted about three hours, and I described the nuances of my life over the preceding three years. I explained the connection between Spence and the Secret Service. I discussed the relationship between Spence and Tony, and elucidated their blackmail enterprise. I named several powerful and affluent men who procured escorts either through me or through Spence, and I edified Van Susteren about the pedophile network that was operated by Spence and King. In addition, I mentioned the threat that had been parsed out to me by a member of George H.W. Bush's cabinet. I handed her credit card receipts, copies of checks, and lists of my clients too.

After I provided Van Susteren with a comprehensive panorama of everything I had witnessed, I was surprised that she didn't seem distressed or stunned by my disclosures. Indeed, she seemed to remain emotionally flat-lined throughout my revelations. She said that she had previously handled sensitive cases like mine in federal court, and she told me that the government would be averse to baring such sordid details in court—she felt that I would most likely end up with probation.

Van Susteren impressed me with her aplomb and also with her quick, snappy answers to my numerous questions, so I left her office feeling a sense of tranquility that I hadn't experienced in months. Later in July, the *Washington Post* published its mendacious, "From Small-Roots, a Big City Scandal," and I reassessed if Van Susteren was the right lawyer for me. After all, a *Washington Post* reporter had steered my mother to her. In fact, the *Washington Post* article left me quite ambivalent about who I should trust, and I reassessed my relationships with just about everyone in my life.

For a few weeks, I tussled with the question of whether or not I should continue to retain Van Susteren, but I ultimately deluded myself into thinking that the *Washington Post* reporter had probably heard of Van Susteren due to her excellent reputation. The stress of my predicament and the negative press had left me emotionally threadbare. I desperately wanted to have faith in her.

Van Susteren and I kept in touch on a regular basis as the grand jury wended into the summer of the following year. After the grand jury had been impaneled for a year, I started to have an extremely uneasy feeling. But Van Susteren repeatedly assured me that I was most likely eyeing probation. She said that if I were indicted, she would make a motion for the government to release a list of my clients, and that would force the government to be reconciliatory towards me.

On the second to last weekend in July of 1990, I flew to Williamson and spent the weekend with my mother, and Van Susteren phoned on Sunday. She said that the grand jury had indicted me, but she wasn't privy to the charges, because it was a sealed indictment. The authorities generally seal indictments to ensure that they're content isn't made public before the indicted suspects are apprehended to safeguard against their flight from the law. I certainly wasn't a flight risk, nor had I given the government indications that I was a flight risk, so I was puzzled by the sealed indictment.

Van Susteren directed me to rendezvous with her at her office the following day. My mother and I awoke at 6:00 A.M. the next morning, and we drove to Washington, D.C. We were extremely anxious about the unspecified charges that were looming over me in D.C., and our drive was marked by a stifling silence. Van Susteren greeted us at her office, and she phoned either Assistant U.S. Attorney Alan Strasser or the Secret Service. She offered to deliver me to the courthouse, but her offer was vetoed, and within 20 minutes four Secret Service agents were standing in Van Susteren's office.

I immediately recognized one of the agents—"Paul Ware." He was about 5'10" and in his late thirties. He had short, dark hair, parted to the side, and an olive complexion. A black suit seemed to loosely drape his stiff, slender frame. Over the preceding months, Ware had routinely and overtly followed me. My mother recognized him too, because he had also followed her.

The Secret Service agents were hostile to me when they arrived at Van Susteren's office, and I felt like they looked upon me as a treasonous enemy of the state. One of the agents flashed a pair of handcuffs, and Van Susteren requested that he cuff me from the front. The agent, however, ignored her request and cuffed me behind my back. The agents then escorted me to a black sedan, and pushed me into the back seat. Two agents sat in the front seat of the car that transported me, and two agents followed us in a second black sedan. As we drove past the White House, Capitol Hill, and DuPont Circle, I experienced a very peculiar sensation. I felt like the Secret Service sedan was suspended in time, and I momentarily had an out-of-body experience as I came to the realization that my life would be forever transfigured.

The Secret Service agents drove me to D.C.'s federal courthouse, and they silently ushered me through the courthouse. After the Secret Service agents booked me, I was deposited in a holding cell that held around 20 inmates. The altered state that I had experienced in the Secret Service sedan was punctured by the harsh reality of the holding cell. I had been in the holding cell for a couple of hours when a pair a U.S. marshals retrieved me. The marshals had the same stern demeanor as the Secret Service agents as they escorted me to a courtroom. As I entered the courtroom, I noticed my mother standing next to an African-American man in his mid-thirties. He was a bail bondsman that Van Susteren had introduced to my mother. The marshals escorted me past my teary-eyed mother to the defense table where Van Susteren stood.

As I sat down, I glanced at Assistant U.S. Attorney Alan Strasser. In addition to overseeing the grand jury that indicted me, Strasser would be in charge of prosecuting my case. The thirty-seven-year-old Strasser was tall and corpulent. He had curly brown hair and a fleshy face that was accentuated by extremely dense eyebrows. He seemed to grimace when we made eye contact. Shortly after I seated myself, Judge Harold Greene strolled into the courtroom. The 67-year-old Greene was short and compact. He had a black comb over, and he wore large brown-framed glasses.

When Judge Greene seated himself at the bench, he leafed through my indictment. Judge Greene was quite surprised that the grand jury had walloped me with a 43-count RICO indictment. RICO is an acronym for the Racketeer Influenced and Corrupt Organizations Act, and it was originally designed to dismantle the Mafia, because RICO allows for mob bosses to be tried for crimes that were sanctioned on their behalf. Judge Greene may have been surprised by my RICO indictment, but I nearly fainted. I was staring at 295 years in a federal prison!

After Judge Greene voiced his astonishment that a mere prostitution case resulted a sealed 43-count RICO indictment, Strasser said something to the effect that my case had special circumstances. Strasser ultimately argued that I should be held without bail, but Van Susteren countered that I wasn't a flight risk, and I had voluntarily surrendered myself shortly after being notified of the indictment. Judge Greene granted me bail, and I was released on a $30,000 surety bond. Judge Greene then mandated that I report to a probation officer once a week, and I had to receive express authorization from him to venture outside of the D.C. area.

Over the course of the hearing, I repeatedly ruminated about the 43-count indictment, and its potential 295-year sentence. After the hearing, I voiced my utter bewilderment to Van Susteren, and she assured me that the indictment was much ado. She reiterated that she felt I was probably eyeing probation. When the hearing concluded, I had dinner with my mother. I said little, because, despite Van Susteren's assurances, I was dumbfounded by the fact that I potentially faced life in prison. Following dinner, my mother drove me to Richard's apartment, and she spent the night with Aunt Josephine. Despite a Xanax, I had great difficulties sleeping. Given my childhood affection for Arnold, I've never been particularly fond of ham, but the federal grand jury was a rather unsavory ham sandwich that I would somehow, someway have to digest.

In the wake of my arraignment, the government walloped Robert, Jimmy, and Travis with multiple RICO counts too. The Secret Service had a list of my clients, but not a single client was indicted. The grand jury also neglected to indict the Secret Service agents who catered to Spence's wishes. Robert, Jimmy,

Travis, and I would be taking the fall for everyone who procured escorts or who engaged in illicit activities with Spence.

As I look back on our predicament, it's obvious to me that the government's draconian treatment of us was designed to leverage our silence. Tony's ploy to have me process credit cards gave the government carte blanche to swarm me with a myriad of RICO offenses.

I had been masterfully set up.

•••

While I was being subjected to the government's Machiavellian malevolence, I also had to contend with the revenge of Michael Manos, who embarked on a check-writing spree with my pilfered identity towards the end of 1988 and into 1989. Manos had vowed revenge, and he was exacting it at a most inopportune time for me. Manos' check writing spree unfolded over D.C., Maryland, and Virginia, and, consequently, I faced various criminal counts in those jurisdictions for passing bad checks.

Manos theft of my identity and his check-forging extravaganza at my expense certainly aided and abetted the government's declaration that Henry Vinson was a miscreant of nearly unparalleled magnitude. I realize that I might provoke incredulity if I speculate that the government may have been well aware of Manos' check forging exploits with my pilfered identity, and it opted to idly stand by as he wracked up offenses in my name. But the *Washington Times* reported that Manos had plundered Paul Balach's checking account for $4,000 and also illicitly used his MasterCard, but the D.C. authorities didn't prosecute Manos for a single count of identity theft or larceny against Paul. Moreover, at that time, I had a nest egg of $500,000, and I was the target of a federal grand jury, so it doesn't make sense that I would run around the D.C. area kiting checks.

Shortly after Manos left D.C., he did a 15-year prison stint in his native New York for kidnapping, robbery, criminal possession of stolen property, and larceny. Following Manos' release from prison, he was strapped with parole for life, but he skipped on his parole. Manos then commenced on a nationwide odyssey of stolen identities, fraud, and embezzlement. He turned up as "Christian Michael de Medici" in Atlanta, where he pedaled a massive mortgage fraud that swindled a bank and private investors.

Once Atlanta became too hot for Manos, he incarnated himself in Dallas as "Mladen Stefanov," media mogul, restaurateur, and scion of a Greek tycoon. After Manos conned and defrauded a wave of marks in Dallas, he fled to California. Federal authorities finally pinched him in San Francisco, and they found 30 phony credit cards and a fake Bulgarian driver's license. He was extradited to New York where he served a year for parole violations, and then he was extradited to Texas where he spent six months in the pokey on fraud charges.

When Manos was released from a Texas jail in June of 2011, he perpetrated his most audacious makeover—a D.C. lobbyist. He wielded a bogus clientele that included big tobacco and the Republican Party. Once more, Manos was arrested and extradited to New York for parole violations. As I've followed the criminal career of Michael Manos, I wasn't alarmed that he impersonated a lobbyist for the Republican Party, because he and Craig Spence had a very cozy relationship, and both were ethical eunuchs.

CHAPTER FOURTEEN

GRETA AND L. RON

I met with Van Susteren at her office shortly after I had been indicted. In addition to facing a lifetime behind bars, I had to cope with the various charges arising from Manos' theft of my identity and his check writing spree. Van Susteren said that she would file a motion that would compel the U.S. Attorney for D.C. to publicly release the names of my clientele, and her motion would abate the government's zealous prosecution of me.

When our conversation rolled around to Michael Manos and his theft of my identity, she suggested that I plea bargain to his offenses and make restitution. Although pleading guilty to Manos' crimes struck me as counter-intuitive, Van Susteren's rationale was that it would be optimal for me to be free and clear of those offenses as she dealt with my 43-count federal quagmire. The angst and apprehension of the preceding year that culminated in my indictments had left me existentially exhausted, and I acquiesced to Van Susteren's recommendations.

As I was in the midst of making restitution for Manos' larceny, I had a status hearing before Judge Greene, which is an informal discussion between the judge, the prosecution, and the defendant about the progress of a case. When I departed the status hearing, I was arrested at the courthouse by Virginia authorities for the various offenses that Michael Manos had committed in Virginia. Secret Service agent Paul Ware was conspicuously present when the Virginia authorities arrested me.

Van Susteren made her vaunted move in the middle of August 1990 by filing an 11-page motion that would force the U.S. Attorney's office to release the names of my clientele, which had been seized by the Secret Service via search warrants and subpoenas, but Strasser stonewalled her motion. He refused to release my client lists, because "he fears intimidation of government witnesses due to the embarrassing nature of the case." The government had been the primary intimidator of my clientele, so I found Strasser's rationale for quashing Van Susteren's motion to be extremely ironic. If the government was unwilling to release the names of my clientele, Van Susteren put forth an alternative motion that would prohibit prosecutors from entering the seized items into evidence for the trial.

In early October, Judge Greene ruled on Van Susteren's motions. He released the documentation to Van Susteren, but he banned its public disclosure. After the ruling, Van Susteren started to undergo a metamorphosis. She eventually advised me to start cooperating with the government. I found her change in strategy to be perplexing. I've since wondered if Van Susteren's maneuver to publicly expose my clientele had been her one-trick pony or if she had sub rosa motivations. By that time, however, I was utterly spent, and I obsequiously complied with Van Susteren's counsel. If she had recommended that I jump off the Empire State Building, I would've booked the next flight to New York.

I ultimately pled guilty to conspiring to violate the Racketeer Influenced and Corrupt Organizations Act and credit card fraud, and I agreed to "cooperate" with government. Although those two counts carried a maximum aggregate sentence of 25 years, Van Susteren assured me that my cooperation would result in a "downward departure" from the sentencing guidelines and probation was the likely outcome.

In addition to persuading Robert, Jimmy, and Travis to cooperate with government, my cooperation entailed a series of debriefings in December of 1990 at the Secret Service's D.C. headquarters. The debriefings were conducted in a nondescript conference room over the course of two weeks. The conference room had tan walls, no windows, and brown indoor-outdoor carpeting. Paul Ware sat at the head of a long, rectangular conference table, and I sat directly to his left. Various men were also seated around the conference table. I was told that they were affiliated with the D.C. Metro Police, U.S. Postal Service, and the Internal Revenue Service, even though my intuition is that they most likely provided false affiliations. As I reflect on my debriefings in retrospect, I find it astonishing that Van Susteren, acting as my attorney, didn't accompany me to a single debriefing. At the time, however, I was very naïve, and I was merely following directions to avoid imprisonment.

Agent Ware controlled the debriefings, and the other men sitting at the table occasionally chimed in with a question, but they were generally taciturn and stoic as they scribbled my statements on yellow legal pads. Ware and his associates seemed to have a rather limited agenda, and, when I offered information that conflicted with their agenda, Ware abruptly stifled me. At first, they wanted to gauge my honesty and relationship with Spence, so Ware asked me if I ever met Spence's wife and children. I replied that Spence wasn't married, and I sincerely doubted that he had children. Ware then asked me specifics about Spence's Kalorama home, which I answered quite thoroughly.

After Ware concluded that I wasn't lying about my relationship with Spence, he started to broach the subject of blackmail. He inquired what I knew of Spence's blackmail activities, and I discussed the concealed bugging equipment that was scattered throughout his house. When I started to offer information about Tony being part and parcel of Spence's blackmail enterprise, I was cut off by Ware. He didn't want to hear about Tony. I then attempted to discuss the pedophilic blackmail enterprise of Spence and King, and again I was thwarted. Ware also stymied me when I started to discuss the cabinet member in the Bush administration who might've been the target of pedophilic blackmail.

Ware was quite interested in the Secret Service agents who were in cahoots with Spence, and he interrogated me about the Secret Service agents I had met at Spence's house. He questioned me about my social interactions with the agents, and I replied that the only time I knowingly interacted with Secret Service officers was at Spence's home. Ware also inquired about the sexual preferences of the Secret Service officer who guarded

Spence, and he asked me if I had ever had sex with a Secret Service agent. The latter question I found to be rather perplexing.

Ware expended hours tossing out names, and garnering feedback on the respective individuals he mentioned. He had a multitude of questions about Paul Balch and Charles Dutcher. Ware asked me where I acquired my presidential cufflinks, and I told him that they were a gift from Paul Balach, and, unbelievably, he inquired about the Truman china. I replied that I had no idea who stole the Truman china. Ware wasn't interested in Tony, who was responsible for innumerable illicit activities, perhaps, even including murder, but the Truman china was of paramount interest to him.

Ware and the panel had numerous questions about an escort named Jeff Gannon, which also perplexed me, because I had only met Gannon on a handful of occasions. Gannon had been an acquaintance of Jimmy's, and I initially met him at Shooters. Although Gannon was an escort, I never employed him. When I talked to Gannon, he maintained he was an escort and a journalist, and he also claimed to be servicing officials in the upper echelons of the Bush administration. He even disclosed that he spent nights in the White House. His stories were quite outrageous, so I didn't give them much credence.

I gave Ware and the panel the limited amount of information that I was privy to concerning Gannon, and I also discussed his extravagant braggadocio. Although I was surprised about Ware's inordinate interest in Gannon, I didn't give it a second thought until fifteen years later when Gannon actually surfaced as a White House reporter. Gannon started attending White House press conferences in early 2003. At the time, he had never published an article, he wasn't associated with a news organization, and he moonlighted as a homosexual escort, but, remarkably, the Secret Service granted him one-day press passes for nearly two years, which enabled him to sidestep the extensive background checks required for permanent passes.

Gannon came under the scrutiny of the White House press corps at a 2005 presidential press conference when he asked President George W. Bush a ridiculously partisan question about the Democrats bleak view of the economy, mentioning that a couple of Democratic senators had "divorced themselves from reality." Bush took Gannon's question quite seriously, giving a protracted response, but it elicited the ire of White House reporters, who started delving into his background, and they quickly discovered that he was a gay escort. By 2005, Gannon ostensibly worked for Talon News, a virtual news service that didn't have a physical office.

The story of Jeff Gannon took an interesting twist after he was outed as a gay escort, because Democrats in the House of Representatives began digging into his connections to the Bush White House. A pair of House members filed Freedom of Information Act requests that inquired about Gannon's access to the White House, and their FOIA requests revealed that Gannon spent a lot of time at the White House. Gannon made over 200 appearances at the White House during his two-year stint as a "White House reporter," attending 155 of 196 White House press briefings. Over a period of tewnty-two months, Gannon checked in with the Secret Service, but he failed to check out on fourteen days, and on one of those days a press briefing wasn't even held.

Although the Secret Service said that there wasn't a "deviation from Secret Service standards and procedures" regarding Gannon's bizarre access to the White House, Democrats on the House Judiciary Committee proffered a resolution that would've required Bush's Attorney General and the Secretary of Homeland Security to surrender documents relating to the security investigations and background checks involved in granting Gannon access to the White House. But Republicans on the Judiciary Committee ultimately overruled the resolution.

The Secret Service was aware of Gannon being a gay escort in 1990, when I was being debriefed, and yet it granted him seemingly unfettered access to the White House from 2003 through 2005. I've always been fascinated by the fact that Gannon failed to check out of the White House on fourteen visitations. So perhaps Gannon was telling me the truth when he said that he actually spent nights at the White House?

•••

After Ware and his colleagues had finished "debriefing" me, I met with Van Susteren approximately once a week. Our discussions gradually began to transcend my legal predicament, and we started to talk about various aspects of our personal lives. Van Susteren eventually told me that she was a Scientologist. I had never met a Scientologist before, so I was both surprised and intrigued by her disclosures about Scientology.

Life has the potential be exponentially stranger than fiction, because in early 1991 I found myself on an Oklahoma-bound flight to Scientology's Narconon rehab, which was located near Newkirk, Oklahoma. Although I've never suffered from chemically dependency, I had a well-founded distrust of the government's intent. So I hoped that graduating from Scientology's Narconon program would demonstrate to Judge Greene that I had made an assiduous effort to turn around my life, and I would receive leniency from him even if the government reneged on its proposed agreement with me.

A Narconon staff member was awaiting me at the Tulsa International Airport, and we drove to northern Oklahoma. Narcanon was housed on the campus of a former boarding school for Native American children that closed in the early 1980s. The campus' yellow limestone buildings were like an archipelago of civilization on the remote, sprawling prairie.

I was aware that Narconon was affiliated with the Church of Scientology, but I didn't realize that the ensuing months would essentially be the D.C. madam meets L. Ron Hubbard on the prairies of Oklahoma. Upon my arrival, I was quickly drenched in the specter and teachings of L. Ron Hubbard. I initially had great difficulties digesting the Scientology dogmas. According to Hubbard, an alien overlord named Xenu was in charge of a "Galactic Confederacy" 75 million years ago that consisted of 76 planets, including Earth. Xenu's planetary confederation was desperately overcrowded, so Xenu devised a genocidal plan. He lured billions of the confederation's citizens to government offices under the pretense of a tax inspection, and he dosed them with paralyzing drugs and flew them to earth, where they were murdered. The souls or thetans of the murdered aliens were then captured and brainwashed, and they eventually incarnated as earthlings.

Although Scientology's theology initially struck me as extremely bizarre, I found the staff nonjudgmental and compassionate, and Narconon was a welcome respite from the inexorable heat I had faced in the government's D.C. pressure cooker. The men and women clients of Narconon had their respective dormitories, but we attended the same classes, which consisted of about 20 clients, and we also communed in the dinner hall. Shortly after my arrival at Narconon, I was assigned an "auditor," who would be the recipient of my deepest and darkest secrets. The auditing process is designed to "clear" Scientologists of their "engrams," which are mental impressions of traumatic events. The auditor records the details associated with an engram, and Scientologists believe that this confession process diffuses the engram's negative affects on our lives.

The Scientologists take being cleared very, very seriously, so I certainly had my work cut out for me while I was in Oklahoma. My auditor, Lawrence, was an elderly man with white hair, and he was a chaperon as well as a confessor. Under his careful supervision, I spent hours and hours writing out my various traumas and transgressions. As my auditing process progressed, Lawrence introduced me to Scientology's E-meter, which measures electrical resistance and skin conductance. An individual's skin conductance varies with his or her concentration of sweat, so skin conductance is used as a proxy for psychological or physiological arousal or stress. As the engrams are diffused through the auditing process, the E-meter theoretically measures less and less arousal and stress. After I had been at Narconon for four months, a Scientology adept whom I had never met decided that I was cleared, and a party was thrown on my behalf. The party was quite festive, and it even included a blue and white cleared cake.

Believe it or not, I actually started to enjoy my hiatus among the Scientologists. The human experience can be fraught with grueling circumstances, and people often grope for credos or belief systems that will gift-wrap their problems with a tidy bow and offer novel solutions. I think that most people experience excruciating impasses in their lives that leave them highly susceptible to various alternative belief systems or cults. At that particular time in my life, I faced an existential crisis that seemed insurmountable and hopeless, and, groping for relief, I was highly susceptible to the pat solutions offered by the doctrines of Scientology.

Although Scientology had declared that I was cleared of engrams, the federal government had yet to decide if I were cleared of imprisonment. A federal probation officer flew out to Oklahoma and conducted a presentence interview, and a few weeks later my presentence report arrived in the mail. I read the report in my dormitory room, sitting on my bed. It recommended a sentence between 63 and 78 months in a federal prison! When I read the presentence report, I was overwhelmed by dread and stunned. A prison stint of five or six years was, apparently, an engram that had yet to be thoroughly cleared, and I immediately phoned Van Susteren. She said that the Justice Department had ruled that I had provided "substantial assistance," and she assured me that I would receive a downward departure from the recommendations in the presentence report.

Judge Greene set June 12th as my sentencing date, so I flew back to D.C. on June 11th. My mother met me at D.C.'s Washington National Airport, and we spent the night at Aunt Josephine's house. The next morning I donned a blue Brooks Brother's suit, white shirt, and a blue tie, and I rendezvoused in the kitchen with my mother and Aunt Josephine. My mother was wearing a tan pants suit and Josephine wore a turquoise pants suit. After breakfast, I drove my mother's car to the courthouse. My mother sat in the front seat and Josephine was in the backseat. Our mood was upbeat, because Van Susteren had said that even if the government slapped me with a six-month sentence, I would be able to self-report to the designated institution at a date specified by Judge Greene.

When we arrived at the courthouse, I rendezvoused with Van Susteren who was standing outside the courtroom, and she had a distressed look on her face. As I had feared, the government decided to pull a dirty trick at the eleventh hour. Shortly before my sentencing, Strasser filed a memorandum with Judge Greene asserting that I should be sentenced *above* the guidelines, because I hadn't screened the escorts I employed for HIV, and thus had perpetrated untold death and misery.

So I was extremely apprehensive as I followed Van Susteren into the courtroom to face Judge Greene. After I expressed contrition for my crimes, Judge Greene launched into a protracted diatribe about the downward departure that had been proposed for my "substantial assistance." "Why propose this departure?" Judge Greene asked. "I can't recall a single case in which the government has asked for departure before just because somebody pleaded guilty and got others to plead ... I don't think it's warranted..."

Van Susteren interjected that I had turned over a new leaf, but Judge Greene brought up the litany of Michael Manos offenses that I had pled guilty to at her behest. He barked out that my offenses included "false checks, false pretenses, theft over a period of years, and plus the long track record in the running of this conspiracy."

My sentencing had suddenly taken on the surreal proportions of a horrific nightmare, and Judge Greene had yet to address Strasser's memorandum about Henry Vinson being the progenitor of the HIV virus in Washington, D.C. Judge Greene asked Strasser if he were aware of anyone who had contracted HIV from an escort whom I employed, and Strasser couldn't mention a single individual, which demonstrated that his memorandum to Judge Greene had been unfounded. Judge Greene then sentenced me to 63 months in a federal prison, and he ruled that I be immediately remanded into custody. As the U.S. marshals escorted me out of the courtroom, my mother was weeping and Aunt Josephine was comforting her.

As I sat in a holding cell, waiting to be transferred to the federal prison in Morgantown, West Virginia, I attempted to decipher the antics that had just transpired in the courtroom and Strasser's eleventh hour memorandum. Trial judges generally have access to law enforcement's debriefing of a suspect, so I wondered if Greene realized the immense scandal I had prevented by plea bargaining and his courtroom antics had been merely grand theater for the press or perhaps the Justice Department and Secret Service had kept Greene in the dark concerning the scope of my cooperation.

I eventually started to drone on about my 63-month sentence to my fellow cellmates, because it seemed like a lifetime to me. The guy sitting next me then snapped that he had just been hammered with an 18-year sentence. I instantly learned the wisdom of silence among the incarcerated.

When Van Susteren was representing me, I thought that she was sincerely acting in my paramount interests, but the government ultimately accomplished its primary objectives: my silence and incarceration. In retrospect, however, I caught a fortuitous break from Judge Greene, because Scientology had nearly purloined my mind, and five years in a federal prison is preferable to a lifetime sentence of Scientology.

CHAPTER FIFTEEN

THE BIG HOUSE

As a teenager, I was horrified of physical education class and locker room pranks. Now I was sentenced to five years in prison, which made physical education class look like a walk in the park on sunny spring day. In addition to the loss of my freedom, I had to contend with the eradication of my individuality. I was stripped of my own clothes, shoes, and even my watch. My name was abruptly reduced to a number—or the generic "inmate." My future quickly became a nebulous uncertainly that I avoided contemplating, because I was solely focused on surviving the present—sometimes day-to-day and sometimes moment-to-moment.

After a week in D.C.'s city jail, I was one of sixty prisoners who were belly-chained, handcuffed, and leg-shackled and escorted to a bus in the jail's basement. When we seated ourselves in the bus, we were chained to our respective seats and then driven to the federal prison in Lorton, Virginia, which served as a transit center for federal prisoners in the D.C. area. The drive to Lorton was less than an hour, and I didn't utter a word while I stared out the bus' barred windows. As I watched the facial expressions of the D.C. commuters driving their cars to work, school, or countless other destinations, I came to the brutal realization that my former life had become null and void.

I was incarcerated at Lorton for three days before again being belly-chained, handcuffed, and leg-shackled and marched to a bus with sixty additional prisoners. We were driven to the federal prison in Lewisburg, Pennsylvania. I was at Lewisburg for nearly a week, and then I was driven to Morgantown with about a hundred other prisoners.

The federal prison at Morgantown was thankfully a minimal security prison, but my reputation as the D.C. madam preceded me. The majority of Morgantown's inmates were privy to my case due to the incessant newspaper reportage on me. The inmate population didn't overtly embrace homosexuals. I was initially treated as an extraterrestrial by many inmates and repeatedly called a "punk," which in inmate jargon is synonymous with queer or faggot. I felt like I was back in high school, but I couldn't escape to my mother's house after school had been adjourned for the day.

My cellmate, Muhammad, was a fiftyish African-American man, who had received a 10-year sentence for the possession and distribution of cocaine. Muhammad hailed from Detroit, and he had spent several years in prison. Although Muhammad sprung from the mean streets of Detroit, I was grateful that he never looked upon me with contempt or hostility. Muhammad also eased my transition to penal life by explaining the unwritten prison mores to me.

I initially had great difficulties sleeping, because I had to listen to my fellow inmates nocturnal snoring and coughing. After lights out at 10:00 P.M., I spent hours tossing and turning every night before I finally managed to drift into sleep. I eventually started to acclimate to the din that ricocheted into my cell on a nightly basis, and my insomnia gradually started to allay.

Every inmate was allotted a "job," and I was assigned to be a cook in the officers' dining room. I quickly learned that the rationale for my assignment was that the inmates weren't receptive to a punk handling their food. Although inmates wouldn't speak to me when we were in general population, a number of them made advances towards me when we were one-on-one. I had been at Morgantown for less than a month when an inmate followed me into the infirmary's bathroom and stood in front of the door. I had a sudden flashback of Jimmy and Rod at Williamson High School. After he attempted to kiss and grope me, I started to scream my lungs out. It was only a matter of time before a guard barged into the bathroom, so he eased off, and I managed to dash out of the bathroom. I regularly experienced those types of incidences during my first three or four months at Morgantown.

As I was departing the officers' dining room one afternoon, a young guard approached me—he was around 28 years old. He exposed himself to me, and he ordered me to perform oral sex on him. When I refused, he said that making a complaint against him would be pointless, because nobody would believe me. I had to cope with prisoners attempting to impose themselves on me, but the thought of guards starting to impose themselves on me was particularly bewildering.

Following my impasse with the guard, I marched straight to the prison's Special Investigative Services (SIS) office, which investigates the activities of inmates and employees, and I made a formal complaint against the guard. SIS conducted an investigation of my accusations, and it ruled in my favor. The guard in question had worked at the prison for a mere four or five months, and he was fired.

•••

My mother rented an apartment in the city of Morgantown, and she visited me weekly. Her visitations were an enormous boost to my morale. Despite my mother's religious beliefs, she had come to the realization that I didn't choose to be a homosexual, but rather I was born a homosexual just as she had been born a heterosexual. She had also come to the realization that Butch and I had fundamentally different personalities, and she relinquished her hopes that I would ultimately grow up to be like Butch. My mother became a fountainhead of unconditional love and support throughout my years in prison, and I'm forever grateful to her.

After three or four months at Morgantown, I eventually started to adjust to my life in stir. Morgantown's recreation room had a piano, and I spent hours playing it. The recreation room had a wide variety of sheet music that included ballads and folk songs that were native to West Virginia, which I taught myself to play. Just as I had retreated to the basement as a child to flee my father's tyranny and play the piano, I retreated to the recreation room's piano to flee the difficulties posed by my fellow inmates. I also devoted hours and hours to reading. I enjoyed reading Robin Cook and Patricia Cornwell mysteries, and I read numerous books on marketing and advertising too.

I eventually befriended an inmate named John, who had been a pilot in the Air Force. Our shared love of airplanes and aviation was the incipient bond that enabled us to forge a friendship. John was tall with thick gray hair and intense blue eyes, and he had a military demeanor that reminded me of Uncle Clarence. John had been a lieutenant colonel in the Air Force, and, following his retirement, he joined the Pennsylvania State Police. John was married, and he had four children. He was busted flying cocaine across the United States, which led to his imprisonment. We dined together every day, and we spent hours talking to each other about everything from flying to the vicissitudes that resulted in our respective incarcerations.

As a funeral director in Williamson, I befriended a member of the West Virginia Board of Funeral Service Examiners, and he was a friend of the prison's "housing manager." The board member I befriended must have spoke highly of me, despite my travails in Williamson, because the housing manager was receptive to cultivating a friendship with me. He eventually assigned me to be the "production clerk" of the prison's onsite factory, which mass-produced furniture.

I oversaw each facet of the factory's production of chairs, tables, credenzas, etc., and I was responsible for ordering every square foot of wood and every screw and hinge that would eventually be modeled into furniture. I have a meticulous nature, whether it be as a funeral director or operating an escort service, so given the intricacies of the job and my painstaking attention to detail and precision, I found the job to be quite challenging, and I poured hours into the task. As I became increasingly focused on the job, my days at Morgantown started to melt away relatively quickly.

•••

Morgantown allowed for a penetrating introspection, and I spent hours pondering the circumstances that had deposited me in prison. I've written this book with years of hindsight, but, when I was initially incarcerated, I had major difficulties comprehending the 43-count indictment and the government's draconian tactics towards my family and me. I also had difficulties understanding why none of the patrons who frequented my escort service were indicted for crimes relating to prostitution. Moreover, after my indictments, I gave the remnants of my escort service to Jeff, my friend and fellow mortician from West Virginia, and he ran the escort service until his death in 2002. Jeff never encountered a single legal problem during the decade or so he operated the escort service.

I now realize that my interactions with Spence, Tony, and King—and knowledge of their perfidious endeavors—were a fait accompli that precipitated my downfall. At the time of my imprisonment, however, I didn't see that causal relationship with the clarity that I see it today, because my last couple of years in D.C. were a nonstop kaleidoscopic montage of nightmares that prevented me from examining my predicament with a modicum of detached introspection.

I was also perplexed by how quickly Van Susteren lost her pizzazz and yielded to the government. I thought I had cultivated a friendship with her, but after my incarceration we never again met face-to-face, even though we talked on the phone as she appealed my sentence. Van Susteren ultimately appealed my sentence on the grounds that the government had offered "a half-hearted, watered down argument" in support of my downward departure despite acknowledging my "substantial assistance." But the appellate court ruled that Judge Greene was the principal arbitrator of my sentence, and he didn't abuse his sentencing latitude with regards to my 63-month sentence. Naturally, the appellate court noted the crimes committed by Michael Manos in my name for an additional reason to justify its decision.

As my doomed appeal wended through the appellate process, I was abruptly called into the SIS office, where I was introduced to a pair of extremely hostile FBI agents. After the FBI agents escorted me to a small room that was adjacent to the SIS office, one of the agents snapped out my Miranda rights. Their intimidating tactics puzzled me, and I was particularly stunned to hear my Miranda rights.

The FBI agents then started to grill me about Illinois Congressmen Dan Rostenkowski and Mel Reynolds. In 1994, Rostenkowski was indicted on corruption charges and Reynolds was indicted for the sexual assault of a sixteen-year-old, obstruction of justice, and solicitation of child pornography. The agents were absolutely convinced that I was privy to the crimes of both Rostenkowski and Reynolds, even though I truthfully told them that I had never met either man, and I wasn't aware of their criminal activity. The FBI agents didn't believe me, so they continued to grill me about Rostenkowski and Reynolds. I certainly didn't want to run afoul of the FBI, but the agents remained incredulous of my repeated disavowals.

Within seventy-two hours of my meeting with the FBI agents, I was charged with inciting a riot at the prison and thrown into solitary confinement. The charge certainly caught me by surprise, because I'm inherently reticent and reserved, and I was especially reticent and reserved while I was in prison. I spent a month in solitary at Morgantown, and it was hellish. I was given a few magazines to read, but that was the scope of my contact with the outside world. Every morning I woke up in a barren cell, and spent the remainder of the day staring at the walls. At times, I felt as if I were on the precipice of losing my mind, so I attempted to transport my mind back to the present as the future seemed like a barren apocalypse.

Following a month in solitary, I embarked on a bizarre odyssey of the federal penal system. I was inexplicably transferred to Lewisburg, which included being piled on a bus with several prisoners, and of course being belly-chained, handcuffed, and leg-shackled. Upon my arrival in Lewisburg, I was thrown into solitary confinement. I was then flown from Lewisburg to the federal prison in Oklahoma City, and I immediately landed in solitary confinement. After a stint of solitary in Oklahoma City, I was flown to the federal prison in Terre Haute, Indiana, where I was immediately deposited in solitary confinement.

While I contended with the hell of solitary at Terre Haute, a pair of guards ushered me to a shower room, and, as I took a solitary shower, a huge African-American inmate also entered the shower room. His face was laden with homicidal intent, and both of us were locked in the shower room. I had nowhere to run, so I cowered into a corner and sat down. The inmate tossed a few glances in my direction, but, thankfully, he left me alone. I was then ushered back to solitary. The federal government can certainly be an unforgiving and malicious foe.

I spent a month in solitary at Terre Haute before I was flown to the federal prison in Manchester, Kentucky, which was a medium security prison. I served the balance of my sentence—18 months—at Manchester. At Manchester, I was mainstreamed into the general population. Although I wouldn't describe the collective mindset of the inmate population at Morgantown to be particularly socially enlightened, they nonetheless seemed Gandhi-like when compared to the inmates of Manchester.

I found that many of the inmates at Manchester were cut from the same cloth as my father's family, and they were plagued by extreme racist and homophobic ignorance. So I primarily kept to myself at Manchester as the days passed like quicksand seeping through an hourglass. My mother continued to visit me on a weekly basis, even though Manchester was a five-hour commute from Williamson.

•••

On July 5, 1995, I was released from Manchester. As I walked out of the prison, I felt the blazing July sun strafe my face, and, peering upwards, I noticed a cerulean sky that was unblemished by clouds. My mother was waiting for me in the parking lot. She wore a lavender pants suit and tears were streaming down her cheeks. When we made eye contact, tears started to well up in my eyes too. She greeted me with a prolonged hug and a labored smile. Although she was eternally thankful that I was being paroled from prison, her smile was labored because my government-sponsored nightmare and its complementary intimidation and harassment had taken a major toll on her. After we hugged, we hopped into her maroon 300 Series Mercedes, and I felt an indescribable euphoria as we drove out of the prison's parking lot.

Following I-79 south through the dense woodlands of West Virginia, we started to discuss my future. I told my mother that I didn't have a definitive plan, because prison, especially my various relocations and bouts of solitary, had reduced me to being primarily focused on surviving the present. She proposed that I manage her ever-expanding real estate fiefdom, and I gratefully accepted her offer. Over the years my mother had become one of the largest real estate proprietors in the Williamson area.

After driving for about four hours, we dined at an Olive Garden in Huntington, West Virginia. Olive Garden isn't exactly Five Star dining, but the capellini pomodoro that I ordered was a delightful departure from years of prison gruel. After dinner, my mother drove me to a federal halfway house in Charleston, West Virginia.

The conditions of my parole mandated six months at the halfway house and three years of probation. The halfway house was a nondescript, two-story house with beige vinyl siding in a lower socioeconomic neighborhood of Charleston. The house's first and second floors had been chopped up into large dormitory style rooms that accommodated ten bunks.

The terms of my parole also required me to find employment. My parole officer abruptly vetoed the idea of me working for my mother. So Dr. Diane Shafer, an orthopedic surgeon who practiced in Williamson, ultimately hired me to be her file clerk. Diane grew up in Pennsylvania, and she had been employed by Appalachian Regional Hospital before entering private practice in Williamson.

Diane had befriended my mother years earlier, and she occasionally spent Saturday or Sunday afternoons lounging around my mother's backyard pool with my mother and her friends. I initially met her when I was 16 years old. Diane was tall with curly brown hair that draped her shoulders. She was brimming with élan, and she had a wonderful sense of humor.

My mother loaned me her Mercedes for the commute between Charleston and Williamson. The three-hour drive seemed like a minor inconvenience compared to federal prison. After I was released from the halfway house, I moved into my mother's house. She had purchased a spacious Tudor home in Williamson that was surrounded by thickets of shrubs and encircled by a white picket fence. Her house in Williamson also had a backyard pool. Over the course of my 9-year absence from Williamson, my mother had developed an affinity for motorcycles, and she had three in her garage, including a Harley Davidson.

I found it extremely difficult to be back in Williamson. Everyone in town was aware of my subsequent fate in Washington, D.C., and again I was treated like a pariah by most of Williamson's denizens. When I wasn't working at Diane's clinic, my early days in Williamson resembled my days at Manchester: I primarily kept to myself and worked out.

Diane eventually expanded her one-physician practice to include four physicians. As Diane was expanding her practice, I started to "manage" my mother's real estate ventures. I put manage in quotes, because my mother was a very headstrong woman and a micromanager, and every business decision, whether it was major or minor, had to receive her blessing. Her metamorphosis from the browbeaten wife of a drunk to a strong-willed, resolute entrepreneur was quite striking.

My mother purchased a two-story building on 2nd Street in Williamson that had previously housed an orthopedic surgery clinic, and she renovated the second floor to accommodate Diane's burgeoning practice. She had the first floor renovated into additional physician offices too, and also into a one-bedroom apartment for me. My apartment had beige walls and beige carpeting, and I garnished its walls with postmodern oil paintings. The living room had an entertainment center that featured a big-screen television, and a sprawling L-shaped sectional couch.

In the months following my release from prison, I had the unsettling sense that the government would, at any given moment, capriciously swoop down on me like a hawk, accuse me of an unsubstantiated parole violation, and toss me back into prison. I was also plagued by nightmares of inexplicably finding myself in solitary confinement. But after a year or so, I started to transcend the omnipresent angst that had shadowed me since the Secret Service raid and throughout my incarceration.

By the summer of 1996, I started to feel that perhaps the government's reign of terror against me had subsided, and I had the self-assurance to purchase a 1989 single-engine Mooney M20, which was fitted with a six-cylinder, air cooled engine manufactured by Porsche. The plane was red, gray, and white, and I thought it was the most beautiful airplane in the world. I had never flown a single-propeller plane that offered such exquisite performance, and whenever I landed the plane, it often attracted on-looking aviation aficionados.

Shortly after I purchased the Mooney M20, I flew to Cincinnati for a weekend visit. At the airport, I bumped into a tall African-American man who was in his late twenties. He had a masters degree in Community Planning, and he was an executive for a hospital in Cincinnati. Although I have tendency to be reticent and coy, I felt an instant attraction to him, and I actually initiated our conversation.

Popular culture is abounding with tales of love at fist sight, but I had never experienced that phenomena. In fact, I was 36 years old, and I had never been in a significant relationship, because that level of interpersonal trust was a seemingly insurmountable obstacle for me. But that day, I truly experienced love at first sight, and I also met a man whose aura of honesty and integrity disarmed my issues with mistrust. He's been my partner since 1996.

As I felt the exhilaration of being in love for the first time in my life, I floated an idea by my mother that was extremely ambitious. A vast building in downtown Williamson, encompassing a city block, had been vacant for a few years. The building had formerly been a clearinghouse for building supplies, and I suggested to her that we convert it into a state-of-the-art rehabilitation center and gym. My mother loved Williamson, and she felt a strong civic obligation, so we embarked on the Tug Valley Rehabilitation Center.

With my mother virtually gazing over my shoulder, I oversaw the gutting of the building and its comprehensive renovation. We designed the facility to offer orthopedic, cardiac, pulmonary and diabetic rehabilitation, outpatient physical therapy, and supervised fitness training. We ultimately equipped it with treadmills, stationary bicycles, rowing machines, Nordic Tracks, StairMasters, elliptical trainers, weights, and a HydroWorx exercise pool. The Tug Valley Rehabilitation Center took about a year to complete, and I felt it was an apt metaphor for my life: I had been existentially gutted, and I was rebuilding my life—bit by bit.

As I was in the midst of overseeing construction on the Tug Valley Rehabilitation Center, the *Charleston Gazette* published an extremely caustic article about me. The article dredged up my incarceration, and it was also littered with unfounded allegations about Diane, including that Diane and I "may" have been married. The article then accused me of faking my death, and it stated that I used the N-word racial epithet when the newspaper's reporter talked to me. The media has never been magnanimous towards me, but that article had an especially vicious sting, because I'm not a racist and my lover is an African-American.

Although the *Charleston Gazette* article rattled me, I continued to forge ahead on the Tug Valley Rehabilitation Center. After the facility's completion, its state-of-the-art features attracted patients from the Williamson area and also from southeast Kentucky. We also charged a monthly fee or a daily fee for the gym. Gyms had previously failed in Williamson, because the area didn't have the populace to support a gym. But housing a rehabilitation center and a gym together proved to be an enormous success.

As the Tug Valley Rehabilitation Center and my relationship flourished, I sincerely thought that I had finally transcended the government's Byzantine machinations that had wreaked such havoc on my life. I even acquired a helicopters license, and I bought a helicopter. My mother absolutely loved helicopter rides in the fall as the rolling woodlands of West Virginia exploded with reds, oranges, and yellows.

One day, however, a journalist who was writing a story about Spence and King and their interstate trafficking of children visited me. I grudgingly met with him to be polite. After we talked for ten or fifteen minutes, he portended that I would be incarcerated within the next couple of years. He told me that I was privy to too many secrets, and I had become too successful and thus credible, so the government would incarcerate me to diminish my credibility. Although he appeared to be quite sane, I nonetheless thought he was crazed: I was leading an exemplary life, and the mere thought of the government incarcerating me again was unfathomable.

Chapter Sixteen

Back to the Big House

In January of 2000, an undulating swarm of approximately 40 federal agents surged into my mother's office building on 2nd Street. The agents were from a collage of federal agencies: FBI, IRS, Medicaid, Medicare, and the U.S. Attorney for the Southern District of West Virginia. They ostensibly made the raid to serve a search warrant on Diane's office, because the government alleged that she had been engaged in fraudulent billing practices. Although the agents ransacked a number of offices, they quickly focused their attention on me.

A handful of agents eventually escorted me to my apartment, and I found myself sitting on my living room's L-shaped sofa with a handful of feds. After we sat down, the investigator for the U.S. Attorney's office and an FBI agent started to grill me. The U.S. Attorney's investigator was in his early fifties, and he had salt and pepper hair. He had menacing grayish eyes, and his taut facial expressions and mechanical mannerisms were that of a Marine boot camp sergeant. The FBI agent was in his mid-thirties, and he had black hair and cutting brown eyes. Both men were tall, thin, and wore the inexpensive suits that I've come to believe are almost mandatory for federal agents.

The agents detained me in my apartment for three or four hours. They said that I wasn't under arrest, but they wouldn't allow me to phone my attorney. Indeed, they wouldn't even allow me to retrieve a glass of water. The agents started the conversation by inquiring about my employment history. I realized that they were alluding to my days in D.C., and I promptly disclosed my former incarnation as a D.C. madam.

The crux of the agents' interrogation pertained to Diane. They said that Diane was overbilling the government and insurance companies, and if I came clean about Diane's billing practices, they were authorized to immediately grant me immunity from prosecution. I told the agents that they had one minor glitch in their supposition: Diane didn't overbill the government or, for that matter, insurance companies. The agents weren't very receptive to the truth, and it made them rather caustic.

The feds' raid quickly ricocheted around Williamson, and my lawyer, who was the former mayor of Williamson, heard that the feds had besieged me in my apartment. So he walked from his office over to my apartment, but the agents wouldn't even let him enter the building. Once more, the U.S. government had mutilated my Fourth, Fifth, and Fourteenth Amendment rights.

After the agents grilled me, they stormed out of my apartment. I was stunned by the agents' harassment, and I felt exhausted after they huffed out of my apartment. Following their departure, I sunk into my living room's couch and stared out the window on the threshold of tears. Although I had been through several hellish ordeals courtesy of the federal government, and I had spent years in federal prison, I didn't have the icy, jaded heart of a hardened ex-con, so the day had left me emotionally tattered.

After the raid on our office building, the U.S. Attorney for the District of Southern West Virginia impaneled a grand jury to supposedly investigate Diane's billing practices, and it started dispensing subpoenas. Given my prior experience, I was acutely concerned about the grand jury's deliberations, but my concerns were assuaged by the fact that I wasn't engaged in any illicit activities. So I genuinely felt that I was exempt from being indicted. But as the grand jury wended for month after month, I started to have flashbacks of being holed up in Richard's apartment as the government prepped my inferno.

A year or so after the feds raided Diane's office, and, as the grand jury was in the midst of its deliberations, I received a phone call from Armando Acosta, a general care physician who had previously leased an office from my mother. Armando was a native of Cuba, and he had a thick accent. He was in his mid-fifties, around 5'8", bald, and morbidly obese.

When Armando initially approached my mother to lease an office, he told her that his medical license had been suspended due to his failure to pay child support, and he was in the midst of financial difficulties. Although my mother was an astute businesswoman, she was also a kind-hearted soul, and she cut a check for his child support arrears and a few of his other outstanding debts. After his medical license was restored, he leased an office from my mother in the same building that housed Diane's clinic, and he moved out of the office about six months after the feds raid.

I hadn't talked to Armando since his exodus from my mother's building, and I was quite surprised to receive a call from him. I consented to rendezvous with Armando, even though I didn't have a stellar opinion of him: I had heard murmurs that he sexually harassed his staff and even his patients. I've been thoroughly skewered by innuendo and falsehoods over the years, so I'm reluctant to judge a man based solely on insinuations, but the numerous intimations swirling around Armando warranted my suspicions.

After Armando phoned me, I met with him in his red, 1960s Pontiac Bonneville convertible. As I took a seat in Armando's car, I noticed he was very edgy, and his eyes repeatedly darted to the left and to the right. Armando had a spicy, bombastic Caribbean persona, but it was eclipsed by his acute agitation. After a few minutes of superfluous small talk, Armando offered me a paper bag that was swollen with $10,000 in cash. He said that the cash was a token of gratitude for my mother helping him to restore his medical license. Armando was parsimonious by nature, so his largesse made absolutely no sense to me. I declined his offer and returned to my office.

Sitting at my desk, I repeatedly ruminated on Armando and his paper bag of cash. I ultimately came to the conclusion that the feds were using Armando to entrap me. The feds using such a transparent ploy was deeply troubling to me, but, conversely, their ploy demonstrated that the grand jury hadn't managed to indict me—yet.

After Armando attempted to entrap me, he was indicted for tax evasion and molesting his patients. In fact, the feds even managed to glean pictures of him molesting patients from an office surveillance camera. Armando was given a sentence of 51 months and sent to prison in November of 2001. The government's game plan had been to use Armando to entrap me, but, given Armando's conviction, I thought it would be nearly impossible for the government to resurrect him as a credible witness. The grand jury, however, persisted with its deliberations.

•••

By the summer of 2002, the grand jury continued to dispense subpoenas. On the first Friday night of July 2002, I had dinner with my sister and mother at my mother's house. My sister looked fatigued, and she complained of a stomach ache. After we helped her to one of my mother's vacant bedrooms, I returned to my apartment. My sister had a massive coronary that night, and my mother found Brenda's lifeless body on the bed the following morning.

On Saturday morning, I received a distraught phone call from my mother, and I raced to her house. Out of breath, I found my mother collapsed on the living room sofa, bawling. Over the years, as a funeral director, I had consoled innumerable grieving mothers, but my mother was inconsolable. When I realized that my words were hopelessly effete, I huddled her into my arms, and, sharing her grief, I also started to sob.

My sister's memorial service was held at Nolan Freewill Baptist Church. My mother, however, was too grief stricken to attend my sister's memorial service and burial. Pastor Ray Taylor was at the pulpit, wearing his customary blue suit, white shirt, and gray tie. Pastor Taylor may have been old and wizened, but he effortlessly launched into fiery oratory.

As Pastor Taylor preached about eternal damnation and the everlasting paradise of heaven, I reflected on my relationship with Brenda. Our personalities and lifestyles were vastly disparate, and that disparity had created a vast chasm between us. She also blamed me for the unbridled vicious-ness that the Secret Service had visited upon her and her hus-band and son—and rightfully so. I had made amends to her on several occasions for the hellish ordeals she had endured due to the Secret Service, even though my amends were re-ceived with lukewarm acceptance. She was also reluctant to visit me during my imprisonment. Brenda ultimately visited me in prison on a handful of occasions, and her visitations were invariably the result of my mother's prodding. We had a friendly, civil relationship, but, as she lay in her coffin, I felt terrible that we had drifted so far apart.

I then found myself reflecting on Butch. Although I had spo-radic reminiscences of Butch, I hadn't intensely reflected on him in years. Butch, Brenda, and I had survived my father's drinking and madness, and that gave us an impermeable bond. I suddenly found myself lost in a montage of memories that included Bren-da playing 45 records and teasing her hair, and Butch driving me out to the airport to fly toy airplanes. The memories were ac-companied by an inescapable anguish and heartache that shad-owed me from Nolan Freewill Baptist Church to Mountain View Memory Gardens, where Brenda was interred. Butch had been interred at Mountain View Memory Gardens 32 years earlier.

Following Brenda's death, my mother skidded into the same abyss of despair that had engulfed her in the wake of Butch's death. She spent days in bed with the curtains drawn. I visited her every day, but she found it nearly impossible to pry herself out of bed. After a few weeks, I was able to coax her to a restau-rant for dinner. As we dined, my mother was nearly catatonic and merely picked at her food.

Just as my mother was starting to marginally recover from Brenda's death, the grand jury indicted me for conspiracy to de-fraud the United States. The government's zeal to indict me was demonstrated by the fact that it had stooped to using Armando, a veritable paragon of honesty and virtue, to finger me as a con-spirator who aided and abetted his income tax evasion. Although the grand jury didn't outright indict my mother, it named her as the "First Known Individual" who played an integral role in the grand conspiracy to succor Armando's evasion of the Internal Revenue Service.

As it turned out, Armando hadn't paid his income taxes for a number of years, so the mere act of my mother (AKA, First Known Individual) cutting checks on his behalf constituted "impeding, impairing, obstructing, and defeating the lawful functions of the Internal Revenue Service..." A major dilemma of the government's case was that my mother and I weren't privy to Armando's outstanding tax problems, even though Armando had spun quite a yarn about how the Vinsons had colluded to abet his income tax evasion. The feds asserted that Diane—not my mother or me—had been sent a letter alerting her of Armando's tax obligations. Diane claimed that she never received a letter from the government, but the government nonetheless maintained that it had sent the letter. The government, however, couldn't provide proof of Diane receiving the letter, because it hadn't been sent via certified mail.

Although my mother was the person who cut the checks to help out Armando, my name was on the company's checking account too—ergo my indictment. But my conspiracy to defraud the United States didn't cease and desist with the checks that my mother cut on Armando's behalf. The indictment claimed that I passed Armando cash after collecting it from his patients and also from various insurers, and I "prepared" false income tax returns for him. The government encountered a couple of hitches with the latter assertions: I never collected cash from Armando's patients, and I've never prepared my own income taxes—let alone Armando's.

The government only indicted me on one count to defraud the United States, but it swarmed me with nine offenses that constituted the indictment, and I would have to defend myself against every one of those offenses. If the prosecutors sowed the seed of beyond a reasonable doubt in the jurors' minds for just one of the offenses, I would be found guilty of the indictment. The feds also named my mother as an unindicted co-conspirator, and I had the disconcerting feeling that they would indict her without hesitation. The outlandish nature of the feds latest indictment, and the deployment of Armando as their star witness, made it quite evident to me that the government was eager to imprison me by any means necessary. Yet again, I felt as if the feds were wielding the Sword of Damocles over my head.

In Washington, D.C., I had a nexus with the Twilight Zone of American jurisprudence. After I had acquiesced to every demand of the Secret Service and the U.S. Attorney, the government double-crossed me with an eleventh hour memorandum that called for me be sentenced above the guidelines for proliferating the spread of HIV. So I ultimately decided to fight the indictment, and I retained a Charleston, West Virginia-based tax attorney.

After my attorney reviewed the case, he was astonished not only by the bizarre nature of the indictment, but also by the great lengths the government took to manufacture it. We poured hundreds of hours into preparing my defense, and a critical facet of my defense would be my mother testifying that she and I were not aware of Armando's prior tax violations. But the Assistant U.S. Attorney for the Southern District of West Virginia told my lawyer that if my mother were called to testify at my trial she would be indicted too. In fact, I had an inkling that if the case even proceeded to trial, my mother would be indicted even if she didn't testify on my behalf. As I've previously mentioned, the federal government can be an unforgiving and malicious foe.

My attorney was new to the Twilight Zone of American jurisprudence, and he was stunned that the feds were threatening to indict my mother. He also saw that my resolve to fight the case was starting to erode once the feds upped the ante to include my mother. My mother had just started to recover from the loss of her daughter, and I couldn't take a chance on her being indicted. When my attorney realized that I would plea bargain to protect my mother, he recommended a strategy that was somewhat similar to the one proffered by Van Susteren. He suggested that I check myself into a detox, so I would be eligible for a downward departure due to the "diminished capacity" of chemical dependency. I was ambivalent about his suggestion, but I reluctantly relented to spend a night in a detox. After all, one night in a detox was infinitely superior to five months at a Scientology boot camp.

After my arraignment, I was released on a signature bond, and I was mandated to undergo urine testing twice a week. During my three years of supervised released, after my first incarceration, I had been urine tested for three years, and I never tested positive for illicit substances. Following my arraignment, however, I had rotator cuff surgery, and I was prescribed a painkiller, and my urine test came back positive for the prescribed painkiller.

Although the feds were aware that I had had surgery the previous week, the assistant U.S. attorneys who were threatening to indict my mother argued that my bond be revoked, because of a "serious continuing drug dependency" that I had "purposely concealed," and my one-night stint at detox was the rationale they cited for supporting their contention. A U.S. magistrate quickly revoked my bond, and I found myself incarcerated at the West Virginia Southern Regional Jail. In retrospect, I should've realized that the government would use everything at its disposal to punish me.

I ultimately entered into a plea agreement with the U.S. Attorney. The judge sentenced me to 41 months in a federal prison. Although Armando had pleaded guilty to tax evasion and also to molesting a number of his patients, he was given a sentence of 51 months—a scant ten months more than me. Once more, I felt that my imprisonment was orchestrated at the highest levels of the Department of Justice.

The media had a field day with my indictment and subsequent plea of guilty. In addition to reporting on my "income tax scheme," the *Charleston Daily Gazette* and *Charleston Daily Mail* recycled previous newspaper reportage on me. Both newspapers, of course, mentioned my days as a D.C. madam. The *Charleston Gazette* called me the "rambunctious former Mingo County coroner." When I ponder various adjectives to describe me, "rambunctious" doesn't immediately come to mind. The *Charleston Gazette* also reported that as the Mingo County coroner I "left a body in an unrefrigerated vault for more than a month" and I also made "harassing phone calls to a former employee." The *Charleston Gazette* was obviously reporting on the impasse with Mr. Marcum's body and the phone calls I had allegedly made to Mrs. Ball, but it couldn't even accurately report on the those apocryphal accounts. So I was subjected to a new wave of media apocrypha.

After my sentencing, I once more embarked on an odyssey of federal prisons. My first stopover was Oklahoma City, and then I was transferred to Lewisburg, Pennsylvania. I was eventually transferred to Morgantown, where I served the balance of my sentence. The first time my partner visited me while I was incarcerated was one of the most humiliating moments of my life, even though he had a box seat as he watched the government railroad me. I felt an unquenchable shame as I greeted him in my government issued orange jumpsuit.

Although I was a seasoned veteran of the prison industrial complex, I found my second incarceration to be extremely more arduous than my first for a variety of factors. First and foremost, my mother was suffering from various ailments, including arthritis and heart disease, and I desperately hoped that she didn't die after outliving two of her children and having a third child in prison. Second, I was unequivocally in love, and it was devastating to be separated from my partner. And finally, I hadn't committed a crime, especially a crime warranting 41 months of imprisonment. At least my prior incarceration had been the consequence of unlawful behavior, even though I was ultimately the fall guy for a sprawling government conspiracy.

• • •

I was released from Morgantown on February 5, 2005. I felt a burst of bliss when my glance grazed the smiling faces of my mother and partner in the prison's parking lot. I gave my mother a protracted hug, and then I gave my partner a protracted hug. The love of mother and partner had never wavered throughout my second bout of American injustice, and I was afloat in a palpable joy as we exchanged hugs. Our parking lot reunion became quite emotional, and a deluge of tears quickly overwhelmed us.

We had a surprisingly upbeat conversation as we drove to the federal halfway house in Charleston, West Virginia, where I was mandated to spend the next six months. Although the circumstances surrounding my second incarceration had been particularly vicious, the government was less draconian with me throughout my second stint of supervised released. After about four months at the halfway house, I was allowed to spend the balance of my federal custody under house arrest in my apartment, and I was even permitted to work for my mother too.

The government may have been less draconian to me during my second stint of supervised release, but, after my second incarceration, I was stalked by an omnipresent angst, because of the well-founded yet disconcerting realization that I wasn't immune to government persecution and imprisonment even if I lived my life by the letter of the law. And as I was transitioning from the halfway house to house arrest in May of 2005, I quickly felt the punitive sting of wayward law enforcement via my mother.

As I lingered in prison, my mother was stricken by severe chest pains and rushed to the emergency room of Williamson Memorial Hospital. The emergency room physician who attended to her was exceptionally attentive and considerate, and he promptly became her primary care physician. My mother thought he was an excellent physician, but the federal government nonetheless charged him with illegally dispensing controlled substances while he was employed at Williamson Memorial Hospital. Although my mother was stunned by the charges, she elected to post a hefty bond for his release, because he lacked a family to post the bond. Thus far, the physician's legal troubles have no relationship to me, except for the fact that he treated my mother and that my mother posted his bond. But rather unsavory behind-the-scenes skullduggery quickly enmeshed me in the predicament.

At the Mingo County Courthouse, my mother offered one of her properties as collateral for the bond. A courthouse clerk wrote that Vinsonian Investments Inc. owned the property although my mother explicitly said that Vinsonian Investments LLC owned the property. After my mother pointed out the clerk's error, the clerk wrote "LLC" over "Inc." Regrettably, the clerk's miscue enabled a crooked West Virginia magistrate to charge my mother with forging the bond agreement, because "LLC" was written over "Inc.," despite the fact that the clerk had changed the document. (In West Virginia, magistrates are elected to office, and they are not required to have legal training, even though they conduct a wide range of judicial proceedings.)

After my mother was charged with forgery, I gave her a ride to the courthouse to resolve the quandary. Mother was suffering from both congestive heart failure and spinal stenosis, so she had great difficulties walking. When I collected my mother at her house, she wore a turquoise pants suit and cradled a portable tank of oxygen. I gingerly helped her into my car, and we embarked for the courthouse. My mother was extremely stressed over the matter, and it exacerbated her shortness of breath. So she hugged an oxygen mask to her face while we were en route to the courthouse. Following our arrival, the Mingo County District Court judge who should've been overseeing the magistrate was conveniently nowhere to be found.

A friend of my mother's, who was a Mingo County Family Court judge, attempted to locate the judge, but he wouldn't respond to her phone calls. My mother then met with the magistrate to resolve the issue. When my stunned mother emerged from the magistrate's office, she told me that the magistrate informed her that her forgery charges would be dismissed if she said that I had forged the bond document! My bewildered mother refused to accommodate him, and he summarily issued a warrant for her arrest.

Shortly after she stepped out of the magistrate's office, she was arrested and handcuffed right in front of me. As she was handcuffed, her facial expressions were disfigured by dread. My mother was being victimized yet again because of me, and I was overwhelmed by scorn. Tears welled up in my eyes, and I exploded with disdain. When I became increasingly vociferous, I was quickly informed that I too would be arrested if I didn't rein in my outbursts. After my mother's arrest, she was transported to the Southwest Regional Jail in Holden, West Virginia, where she was strip searched and thrown into a jail cell. In a frenzied state, I raced to the Southwest Regional Jail, and I posted her bond. Although she only spent about four hours in jail, the experience was traumatizing to her. My mother's case was ultimately brought before a magistrate who wasn't corrupt, and he dismissed the charges.

The *Charleston Gazette* had a field day with my mother's arrest. The first sentence of the article mentioned my mother and noted my "guilty plea to federal charges in 2003 kept her from facing trial ..." Predictably, the article commented on me pleading guilty to racketeering for the operation of a Washington, D.C. escort service, and, of course, it remarked on the apocryphal story that I left Mr. Marcum's body "unrefrigerated" for forty-two days. When the charges against my mother were dismissed, the *Charleston Gazette* ran a terse write-up about her exoneration that was buried in the deep recesses of the newspaper.

My trials and tribulations have demonstrated to me that truth and the reality manufactured by the media are often diametric, because the truth is frequently obscured by a levy of lies. From time to time, however, the levy harnessing the lies eventually cracks, and torrents of truth flood into the public consciousness—albeit belatedly. The truth about the utter corruption of the judge and magistrate who contrived my mother's arrest eventually emerged, but, unfortunately, it was years after the fact.

The corrupt judge who was the architect of my mother's arrest had an affair with his married secretary, and, when she extricated herself from the affair, the judge conscripted a West Virginia state trooper to plant drugs on her husband. The state trooper balked at his scheme, but he was willing to arrest the husband on trumped up larceny charges. The Mingo County prosecutor was cognizant of the affair, and he recused himself from the case, which would have led to the appointment of a special prosecutor who might have uncovered the judge's maniacal scheme, so the larceny charges against the beleaguered

husband were eventually dismissed. After the judge's second attempt to imprison the husband was thwarted, he hired a couple
of heavies to pummel the husband, and the judge then charged
the husband with assault.

On the two occasions the husband was arrested—for larceny
and assault—Magistrate Eugene Crum signed the arrest warrants, and Crum just happened to be the same magistrate who
had my mother arrested. Magistrate Crum would eventually
become the Mingo County Sheriff, and a 37-year-old man who
claimed that Crum had molested him as a teenager murdered
him. Prior to becoming a Mingo County magistrate and the
Mingo County Sheriff, Crum was the sheriff of a small town in
southeastern West Virginia, where he allegedly raped a 19-year-
old woman in the backseat of squad car while two of his subordi-
nates sat in the front seat of the car. A few hours after the alleged
rape, the woman arrived at the emergency room of Williamson
Memorial Hospital, where she told the staff she had sustained
injuries during the rape. But after the young woman was subjected to a succession of threats, she withdrew her rape allegations against Crum, and the West Virginia State Police cleared
him of the rape. I would be remiss if I didn't mention that Crum
and Dr. Armando Acosta were very close friends.

Joyce Vinson at her Merle Norman Cosmetic Studio

CHAPTER SEVENTEEN

A THIRD ACT

F Scott Fitzgerald wrote that America is a country that doesn't grant second acts. Although Fitzgerald wasn't granted a second act, Americans have granted numerous sports stars and entertainment personalities second acts after they've been enmeshed in various personal and legal troubles. However, I felt a small town like Williamson would never grant me a third act, and upon my release from prison my problems with Magistrate Crum sanctified my suspicions.

I was also distressed by the wave of malicious press that had skewered me prior to my second incarceration. The West Virginia media had so spitefully blighted my name that I longed for the anonymity that a larger city would offer me. Over the years, believe it or not, I've been almost as troubled by the media's pernicious portrayal of me than by the government's pernicious persecution. So as I was incarcerated at Morgantown, I grappled with the question of whether or not I should relocate to Cincinnati after being released from federal custody.

When my mother visited me in prison about a year before my release, I broached the subject of my prospective move to Cincinnati. I didn't want her to feel abandoned, and I told her that I wouldn't make the move if she felt that her waning health necessitated that I live in Williamson. But to my utter astonishment, my mother not only supported my move to Cincinnati, she said that she would think about relocating to Cincinnati herself. Although my mother was extremely ambivalent about moving to Cincinnati, because she was so enmeshed in her church and circle of friends in Williamson, the trauma she suffered at the hands of Magistrate Crum was the critical mass in her decision to relocate.

At the conclusion of my house arrest in August of 2005, I made the move. By 2005, my mother's real estate fiefdom encompassed properties in West Virginia, Pennsylvania, Maryland, Virginia, and southern Ohio. She owned several buildings in Cincinnati and also two adjacent townhouses. My partner and I moved into one of the townhouses in August, and my mother followed a month later, moving into the adjacent townhouse.

My first month or so in Cincinnati was a whirlwind of activity. I oversaw my mother's move too. And I enrolled in an online master of science in integrated marketing communications program offered by the University of West Virginia. The program consisted of five nine-week terms, and it was very labor intensive. So between acclimating to Cincinnati and my coursework I kept very busy.

I had to check in with my federal probation officer once a month too. My probation officer in Cincinnati was a tall, lithe blonde with sparkling blue eyes who was in her late thirties. She wasn't cast from same jaded, misanthropic mold as many of her colleagues that I had previously encountered in the prison industrial complex. She had a master's degree, and she encouraged my pursuit of a master's degree. She also concluded that my depiction by the government and media as a criminal mastermind and hardboiled sociopath were fabrications built on fabrications, lacking a foundation of truth, and she terminated my probation two years early.

My earlier incarnation in Cincinnati, when I attended the Cincinnati College of Mortuary Science, had been an enchanting chapter in my life: I was a naïve young man from an isolated corner of West Virginia who was the quintessence of innocence and Cincinnati was an intimidating metropolis. Those two years were teeming with awe and exhilaration as I attended college, explored my nascent sexuality, and pursued my pilot's license. I felt like life was a magical canvas, and my dreams would be the brush strokes and colors that painted a wondrous picture.

In my second Cincinnati incarnation, the awe and exhilaration had been fleeced from my life, and the magical canvas that

I thought would be transformed into a Vermeer or Degas now resembled a painting by Edvard Munch. Since my departure from Cincinnati in 1982, my innocence had been lost, both figuratively and literally. I had been the prime mover in the loss of figurative innocence, and I had also played an integral role in the loss of my literal innocence in Washington, D.C. But the government had manufactured my second incarceration, and I felt the latter persecution had vanquished me to being irredeemable in the eyes of society.

Upon my return to Cincinnati, I needed to somehow forge a détente of sorts with my past and embark on a new life for myself. In addition to the unconditional love of my mother, I also had the unconditional love of my partner. He had remained faithful while I was incarcerated, and I was extremely grateful for his resolute devotion to our relationship. Although my life had been blessed by both material security and unconditional love, the emotional lacerations I'd suffered over the preceding 15 years had left indelible psychological scars, and a pervasive sense of trepidation as I awaited the government's next salvo of persecution.

•••

Before my mother relocated to Cincinnati, she had surgery for spinal stenosis. The results of her surgery were less than optimal, and she required an electrical cart to traverse distances longer than 100 feet. She was also immersed in constant pain. Although her arrival in Cincinnati was a wellspring of merriment for my partner and me, I could see that she was having significant difficulties coping with her ambulatory struggles and her mounting physical discomfort.

My mother dearly loved my partner and vice versa, so the three of us spent innumerable hours together every day. My mother also developed an affinity for my bull terrier—Big Daddy. I was surprised that she developed such an affinity for Big Daddy, because overall she wasn't exceptionally fond of canines. At night, my mother, my partner, and I often dined out, and I thought she was making a smooth segue from Williamson to Cincinnati. But after she had resided in Cincinnati for only a month, she started to become extremely depressed. She had never fully transcended the grief of my sister's death, and she started to long for her friends and church in Williamson. As my mother's emotional state deteriorated, my partner and I made a concerted effort to ensure that she was never alone.

Despite our efforts, we found it impossible to assuage her downward emotional spiral. After she had been in Cincinnati for a couple of months, she voiced her decision to return to Williamson. She and I were sitting at her kitchen table holding hands. I desperately wanted my mother to pass her waning days in close proximity to me, and I told her that I would return to Williamson too, but she vetoed the idea with a wave of her hand. She was adamant that I assemble a new life for myself in Cincinnati.

After my mother's return to Williamson in November of 2005, I phoned her every day, and I also flew to Williamson on a weekly basis. Although she was among her friends and attending her church every Sunday, her depression became even more stifling and suffocating as winter retreated to spring. One day in May, she told me that she wanted to drive her electric cart into the pool. My mother losing her will to live was devastating to me, because she been such an inexorable pillar of strength for me throughout my life.

In June, my mother phoned me, and she complained of severe chest pains. After I hung up the phone, I promptly called Williamson Memorial Hospital, which dispatched an ambulance to her house, and I flew to Williamson that afternoon. Surprisingly, when I arrived at the hospital, I found my mother in great spirits. Her chest pains had merely been a bout of angina, and she told me that she had made a conscious decision to cease wallowing in despair.

As I flew back to Cincinnati that night, I felt a great relief that my mother's chest pains were merely angina, and that she had recovered her will to live. But the following morning, I received a call from Williamson Memorial Hospital. My mother's physician relayed to me she had a bowel obstruction, and she was in septic shock. Her physician also told me that she should be transferred to Cabell Huntington Hospital in Huntington, West Virginia, via a medevac helicopter, for the surgery. I instantly consented to the transfer.

After talking to my mother's physician, I raced to the airport and made the 40-minute flight to Williamson. As I started my descent into Williamson, I noticed the medevac helicopter flying towards Williamson Memorial Hospital. Once I landed, I hopped into the car I kept in the airport's parking lot and sped to the hospital. The hospital's helicopter port was located in its parking lot, and, as I pulled into the parking lot, my mother was being transported to the helicopter in a hospital gurney. I leapt from my car and sprinted over to the gurney. My mother was unconscious and her complexion was ashen.

The helicopter personnel wouldn't allow me to make the flight to Huntington aboard the helicopter, so I zipped back to the airport and flew to Huntington. I rented a car at Huntington's Tri-State Airport, and I darted to Cabell Huntington Hospital. After I dashed into the hospital, I was directed to my mother's attending physicians.

Her physicians weren't optimistic about her prognosis. They said that she required a colostomy, but, given her significantly weakened physical state, there was a high probability that the surgery might result in her death. Conversely, if she didn't have the surgery, she would surely die. I felt my only option was to unhesitantly acquiesce to her surgery. The five-hour surgery seemed interminable as I paced back and forth in the hospital's lobby.

My mother survived the operation, but, during the surgery, she suffered a stroke that left her partially paralyzed and unable to walk. Once she was stabilized, I had her airlifted to Christ Hospital in Cincinnati, because I thought that Christ Hospital offered an excellent rehabilitation facility, and she began her slow, painstaking physical rehabilitation. I spent hours with her every day, and it was truly heartbreaking for me to see her so infirmed. After she had been at Christ Hospital for about a month, she repeatedly expressed her wish to return to Williamson.

When her physicians at Christ Hospital determined that her rehabilitation had progressed to a stage where they thought she could return to her home, I arranged for her to have a 24-hour health care attendant, and I flew her to Williamson. She was extremely debilitated, so I decided to spend the next couple of weeks with her before I returned to Cincinnati. She passed away, in her bed, after she had been home for a week. In retrospect, I think that she realized her death was imminent, which fueled her insistence to return to Williamson.

I also intuited that her death was imminent when she was at Christ Hospital. But I subconsciously muffled that intuition, because the thought of life without my mother was incomprehensible to me. After her death, a smothering darkness encompassed me like molten tar. I felt a loneliness and barren desolation unlike I had ever experienced—a loneliness and barren desolation that easily eclipsed the desolation I felt in solitary confinement.

The night my mother died, I phoned my partner, and he flew to Williamson the following day. Although I consciously knew that I could take solace in my partner's love, the loss of my mother nonetheless made me feel like I was all alone in a cruel, unforgiving world. My soul felt like shards of broken glass as I made preparations for her viewing and memorial service.

My mother's viewing was held at a funeral home in Belfry, Kentucky, and, prior to the viewing, I had a few hours alone with her. She was buried in her favorite pants suit, which was aqua colored. As I stood before her coffin, I profusely apologized for the boundless suffering and abuse that had marred her life due to me. I certainly didn't intend to be the fountainhead of my mother's inordinate suffering, but I felt the greatest mistake she ever made was giving birth to me. I had assiduously attempted to make a living amends to her, and now that she had passed I would continue that amends by donating to various churches and charities that were important to her.

The next day my mother's memorial service was held at Bethel Temple Assembly of God in Williamson. My mother had drifted away from Nolan Freewill Baptist Church years earlier, and she had become a parishioner at Bethel Temple, which had been built in 1996. The church was a cavernous, modern-style brick building that was atop a remote hill on the outskirts of Williamson.

My partner and I arrived at Bethel Temple an hour before my mother's memorial service, and the pastor gave us a warm, sympathetic greeting. The pastor was a tall, lumbering man in his fifties who wore a navy blue suit. He had a benign, oblong face with soft blue eyes, and receding gray hair. Although I was mired in grief, I was also extremely apprehensive about how the congregation would receive me. I had no doubts that all of the church's parishioners were aware of my infamous past. I expressed my concerns to the pastor, and he assured me that the congregation would treat me as if I were part of their extended family. Indeed, the church's parishioners were extremely thoughtful and compassionate to me. I felt a genuine love emanating from the 200 or so mourners who attended my mother's memorial service.

The memorial service, however, was a surreal blur to me. I thought that I had attained a modicum of reconciliation with my mother's death the previous day at the funeral home, but her memorial service engendered relentless surges of sorrow and regret. Although I periodically glanced upward towards the pastor as he delivered the eulogy, and I noticed his gesticulations, his words were virtually inaudible to me. The surges of sorrow and regret accompanied me to Mountain View Memory Gardens, where my mother was laid to rest—next to Brenda and Butch.

♦♦♦

An unyielding gloom descended over me for months after my mother's funeral. I was in the habit of phoning her at least once a day, and on multiple occasions I found myself on the verge of reflexively phoning her before abruptly realizing that she had passed. We discussed issues in our lives that were both meaningful and meaningless and also relevant and irrelevant, and I unvaryingly phoned her when I faced daunting difficulties. And less than a year after her death, I faced an extremely daunting difficulty: the IRS unleashed a three-year audit on me.

As I've previously mentioned, after my second incarceration, I've been stalked by an omnipresent angst based on the realization that the government could indiscriminately deposit me in prison at its whim, and I sincerely thought that the audit was the government attempting to incarcerate me yet again. Perhaps I'm paranoid, but, given my prior travails, I don't think it's necessarily irrational for me to think that I'm perpetually in the government's crosshairs.

The "random" IRS audit began in 2007, and it concluded in 2008. The audit was initially slated to cover my taxes for 2006, but, after the audit vindicated me for 2006, the IRS decided to continue its excavation into my finances, so the audit ultimately covered 2004 and 2005 too. I was slightly perplexed when the audit augured into the years when I was in prison, even though, in retrospect, I should have expected the government to exercise its due diligence concerning Henry Vinson. In 2008, the audit unequivocally cleared me of any and all transgressions against the IRS for the years 2004, 2005, and 2006.

My life was surprisingly devoid of government-contrived pyrotechnics and media assaults over the next four years, and the omnipresent angst that had stalked my life for years started to wane, even though it never quite vanished. I was intensely motivated to participate in mortuary services once more due to my reverence and understanding of the industry, but the West Virginia Board of Funeral Service Examiners refused to even consider my licensure. I had one appellate option, which was to the judge who orchestrated my mother's arrest, so my appeal was ultimately an exercise in futility.

Although I had abandoned all hope of becoming a licensed funeral director, I owned four buildings in Cincinnati that had been converted into funeral homes. I leased three of the buildings to one mortuary service, and I leased the fourth building to a second mortuary service. The two mortuary services that leased buildings from me also contracted my services as an advertising and marketing consultant, and I consulted for two other funeral homes that didn't lease space from me.

I also bought a building in Indianapolis, and I had it converted into a funeral home. I leased the Indianapolis building to a funeral service based in Indiana, and it contracted my consulting services too. I eventually sold the building in Indianapolis to a national chain of funeral homes, and the sale was seamless.

I mention that the Indianapolis sale was seamless, because I wasn't so fortunate with a similar transaction less than a year later. The funeral service that leased three of my buildings sold a number of its assets to a second national funeral chain, and I also sold the chain the three buildings that had housed the funeral service. The funeral service had primarily catered to Cincinnati's African-Americans, and I offered my consulting services to the national chain that purchased the service's assets, because of my prior marketing successes.

The funeral chain flew me to its Midwest headquarters, and I met with a handful of the company's executives, including its president. I presented various marketing ideas to them. Prior to our meeting, I purchased five domain names that were based on variations of the company's name, and I showed the executives how the domain names could enhance their marketing capabilities. The chain ultimately opted not to contract my consulting services, so I never used the five domain names, and I also relinquished their ownership.

I think I could have been of great benefit to the national chain as it entered the Cincinnati market, because it lost a significant market share compared to the market share of the funeral service whose assets it had acquired. The national chain eventually sued me over the domain names that I had never used and also relinquished. Although the lawsuit was initially initiated over the domain names, it then mutated into a myriad of other issues. The president of the national chain has referred to me as a "lawless individual" as he's beset me with litigation.

As the national chain enmeshed me in litigation, *Funeral Service Insider*, which is the premiere trade magazine for the funeral industry, started to run a series of articles on me that were far from charitable. Indeed, the first article's headline read: "Convicted Felon's Connection to Cincinnati Funeral Home Questioned," and the subheadline was particularly unflattering: "Former Prostitution Ring Kingpin and Ex-Swindler Says He's Just a Landlord." I had moved to Cincinnati to live out the balance of my life in anonymity, but unfortunately I discovered that escaping my past was an impossibility.

In fact, *Funeral Service Insider* gorged on the negative press that I had received over the years. The magazine's six-article hatchet job on me dedicated profuse verbiage to discussing my imprisonment for running a "prostitution empire and conspiring with a doctor to hide money from the government." The articles commented on my reported welfare fraud, my storage of an unrefrigerated body, and of course my "phone harassment" of a former employer. Given the seemingly endless parade of apocrypha that's been mass-produced about me, it's effortless to custom tailor a deconstruction of my character, but I thought six articles had a tendency to be overkill.

Although I've grudgingly acclimated to being maligned by the media, I found one of the articles to be particularly vexing, because *Funeral Service Insider* didn't have the nominal decency to omit my mother from its hatchet job. The magazine reported on her arrest for "submitting forged documents to the circuit clerk's office" when she bailed out her physician. The article never delved into the actual truth behind her arrest.

As I was being besieged by *Funeral Service Insider's* character assassination and by litigation with the national funeral chain, the government, regrettably yet predictably, renewed its persecution of me. An assistant U.S. Attorney for the District of Southern West Virginia, who played an integral role in my 2003 imprisonment, shifted her attention to physicians and pharmacies that were unlawfully dispensing narcotics.

In her fervor to prosecute me, she threatened a West Virginia physician with the loss of his medical license if he didn't finger me as a conspirator in the illegal prescription of narcotics. Her plan, however, had a couple of minor glitches: the physician in question had never met me, and he surreptitiously recorded her threats. When the physician exposed her malevolence, she was booted out of the Justice Department.

But the government wasn't about to be deterred by that mishap, because it yet again raided the building of physician offices in Williamson that my mother had once owned, and the feds once more impaneled a grand jury to probe the physicians' illicit writing of prescriptions. Needless to say, grand juries haven't been particularly benevolent to me, so I felt an acute aftershock when I heard that a grand jury had been impaneled.

Theoretically, I shouldn't have had concerns about the grand jury probe, because, after my mother died, I had sold the properties in Williamson that she left me. I wanted to divest of them right after she passed in 2006, but they were initially gridlocked in probate court, and then the IRS audit further gridlocked their sale. When the IRS finally cleared me of crimes to defraud the United States in 2008, I divested of my Williamson properties in 2009.

I sold four properties, including a surgical center and two buildings that housed physician offices, to a woman who was the office manager for one of the physicians' practices, and the feds ultimately charged her with the misuse of a Drug Enforcement Agency registration card. She was facing four years in prison, and she was almost certainly attempting to reap a reduced sentence, because she implicated me in her schemes. The only problem with her ruse was that I had zero involvement with the clinic after I sold the properties to her. My only connection to the clinic came after the feds swooped in on her for the misuse of a DEA card, and she stopped making her mortgage payments, so the properties' ownership reverted back to me.

The government, however, has never been deterred by reality when it's prosecuted me, and I started to hear rumblings that I would be indicted, even though I didn't have a clue about the scope of the indictment. As I awaited my enigmatic yet seemingly impending indictment, my attorney was contacted by the office for U.S. Attorney for the District of Southern West Virginia. The prosecutors inexplicably sought to issue a press release that stated I had forfeited the building that had housed the clinic, and that the government had taken possession of it.

I found the U.S. Attorney for the District of Southern West Virginia's proposal to be rather baffling. The government wanted me to relinquish a $1 million building without offering a promise that it would cease and desist in my prosecution for crimes that it had yet to specify I had committed. The U.S. Attorney for the District of Southern West Virginia eventually amended its arrangement and proposed that if I forfeited the building, it wouldn't prosecute me for crimes that were still unspecified.

I ultimately caved in to the government's extortion and relinquished the building, because my government sponsored trials and tribulations have left me exhausted. In return for the building, my attorney received a three-sentence letter, and the last sentence reads as follows: "I wanted to write to inform you that the investigation into those matters has been concluded with respect to your client, and no further action is being taken by this office thereon concerning your client."

Welcome to American justice à la Henry Vinson.

CHAPTER EIGHTEEN

SONGS OF EXPERIENCE

As I contemplate my life in retrospect, I've concluded that it has the hallmarks of a contemporary, made-in-America Shakespearean tragedy. When I was a young man growing up in Nolan, West Virginia, I embarked on a noble calling that would assuage the suffering of the bereaved, but the vagaries of fate intervened the day I crossed the threshold of Shooters, and I ultimately made an ill-fated decision that triggered a cascade of events, resulting in disaster and disgrace. Indeed, I have great difficulties believing how my life has unfolded, even though I've had a front row seat to the tragedy.

Shooters was essentially a wormhole that transported me to a dark, foreboding constellation of power politics and blackmail—a constellation that was previously as unfathomable to me as it is to most Americans. In the first chapter, I mentioned that Americans have a collective naiveté about D.C. sex scandals. They have a tendency to believe that they're the isolated dalliances and the moral failings of a handful of individuals—such as Bill Clinton or Eliot Spitzer. Americans have great difficulties accepting that many of our alpha male politicians are endowed with an intoxicating alchemy of power, arrogance, and lust that fluently translates into extramarital affairs or, in extreme cases, the sexual exploitation of minors—like Mark Foley.

Unfortunately, I was the fall guy when the government determined the time was right to cover up the criminal exploits of Spence et al. A troubling aspect of Spence's shadowy network is that the CIA's fingerprints are seemingly visible when the veil is lifted. Spence was a CIA asset, and CIA Director William Casey and former CIA agent and Bush national security advisor Donald Gregg seem to have been enmeshed with Spence too. I've also commented on the *Washington Post's* connections to the CIA.

A second troubling aspect of Spence et al. is the breathtaking federal power that was arrayed to cover up Spence's criminal activities, which give credence to my belief that Spence's exploits were affiliated with government. The feds deployed the Justice Department and Secret Service to erase the slightest vestiges of Spence's criminal enterprise, and of course the *Washington Post* ultimately stamped its imprimatur on the cover up. Although I primarily dealt with Spence, I think that King's involvement in the pandering and blackmail enterprise illustrates the network's transcontinental scope and the breathtaking federal power that was arrayed to seal its cover up.

A Nebraska senate subcommittee investigated King's interstate transportation of children, because Nebraska's law enforcement had ignored the pleas of Nebraska's social services. Unlike in Washington, D.C., where politicians were mum about the exploits of Spence, the Nebraska senators were relentless as they pushed to uncover the exploits of King. But both a state and federal grand jury in Nebraska declared that King wasn't involved in the abuse or pandering of a single child. So ultimately, three grand juries were required to cover up the network of Spence and King—two in Nebraska and the one in Washington, D.C. I've shown that it's relatively straightforward to hijack a grand jury if its special prosecutor is in on the fix, but the hijacking of three grand juries demonstrates breathtaking power.

I've also found it rather interesting that the some of the individuals who played an instrumental role in either ensuring or abetting my silence have experienced remarkable upward mobility. For example, Jay Stephens, the U.S. Attorney for the District of Columbia, whose office oversaw the corrupt grand jury that walloped me with a potential sentence of 295 years, was appointed United States Associate Attorney General by President George W. Bush in 2001. But Associate Attorney General proved to be a two-year pit stop for Stephens, because in 2002 he became a vice president of the Raytheon Corporation, the world's fifth largest defense contractor, and also the world's leading producer of guided missiles.

Greta Van Susteren has experienced a sharp upwardly mobile trajectory herself since I was initially imprisoned. Shortly after Judge Harold Greene banished me to federal prison, Van Susteren started co-hosting CNN's *Burden of Proof*, and then she hosted CNN's *The Point with Greta Van Susteren*. Greta made her vaunted leap to FOX in 2002, where she's been transformed into a media superstar, hosting *On the Record with Greta Van Susteren*. I'm slightly perplexed that FOX, a news outlet that caters to religious and conservative Americans, would elevate a Scientologist to its pantheon of superstars.

In the first chapter, I discussed the misfortunes of Deborah Jeane Palfrey, who assumed the mantle of "D.C. madam" after I had been ignominiously toppled by the government, and I commented on the various parallels in our respective cases. The death of Palfrey has been mired in mystery and speculation due to the anomalous circumstances surrounding her suicide, even though the *Washington Post* was quick to pronounce her death a suicide. Because of the *Washington Post's* deceitful reporting on the tangle of intrigue that ensnared me, and also the newspaper's extensive connections to the intelligence community, I'm extremely reluctant to embrace any of its pronouncements.

Although I'm unwilling to speculate if Palfrey's death was a suicide or a murder, I absolutely believe that if I had let my case proceed to trial and exposed the illegalities that I had personally witnessed in Washington, D.C., I would've been murdered. I realize that my latter statement may sound farfetched or, perhaps, even preposterous, but I have no doubts that the shadowy enclave that engaged the services of Spence, King, and Tony to carry out its nefarious schemes are quite capable of murder, and they wouldn't have hesitated to murder me if I started to spill their secrets. After all, it had no compunction about destroying the lives of children, so it wouldn't harbor second thoughts about murdering a mortician from West Virginia.

The majority of Americans have come to the painful realization that their government has pockets of corruption, but they don't have an inkling of its vast scope. Americans most likely think that the torrents of cash that flow from special interests to politicians are solely responsible for the corruption of their body politic, and they don't realize that blackmail plays an integral role in the usurping of their democracy too.

I feel that Larry Craig is an example of a congressman who was possibly compromised. Craig was in Washington, D.C. for nearly 30 years as a U.S. representative and a senator, and he brazenly solicitied sex from my escort service and also brazenly solicited sex in a public restroom. Given Craig's status as a conservative Republican, if word of his shadow life leaked out, it would result in political suicide and public disgrace, but his runaway libido compelled him to take mindboggling risks.

I find it nearly impossible to believe that Craig's homosexual exploits were unnoticed by the shadowy cadre who were enmeshed with Spence and Tony, because of my belief that they were aware of the patrons who used my escort service. I'm also of the belief that the foremost explanation that can be offered concerning Craig's brazen exploits with regards to his homosexuality is that he was compromised, and he was mindful that his brazen exploits would be covered up. In the first chapter, I mentioned that the federal government has a greater dexterity to cover up scandals and crimes that lend themselves to blackmail in D.C. due to the fact that the capital's law enforcement is exclusively controlled by various branches of the federal government. Perhaps Craig strayed out of his protective net when he attempted to solicit sex in a public restroom at the Minneapolis-St. Paul International Airport?

As I mentioned earlier in the book, the cabinet member who administered a threat to me on behalf of Spence when I balked at covering for Donald Gregg with the Government Accounting Office must have been in the same shadowy network as Spence, or that shadowy network was blackmailing him. Otherwise, it doesn't make sense that he would jeopardize his exalted status and family to abet an utter lunatic and psychopath who's in the midst of a free fall crack addiction.

I think Americans are clueless about the endemic blackmailing of their politicians, because many of their media pundits have probably fallen prey to blackmail themselves. A number of media superstars used my escort service, and it's within the realm of reason that they too became victims of blackmail. I don't necessarily believe that a powerbroker, and media superstars are certainly powerbrokers, who had dalliances with the escorts I employed had to attend Spence's parties to be compromised. The shadowy network that was composed of Spence, Tony, Secret Service agents, most likely CIA agents, and only God knows who else were definitely monitoring my phones and certainly my financial transactions. So I believe a patron who merely phoned me had the potential to become a blackmail target. The media pundits who used my escort service are alive and thriving in their respective milieus, and since the Secret Service absconded with the documentation that demonstrates they procured escorts from me, I can't name them without threat of a lawsuit.

Dr. Vernon Houk quickly comes to mind when I think of a patron of my escort service who may have fallen prey to blackmail. Houk served as the Director of the Center for Environmental Heath at the Centers for Disease Control and also as the Assistant Surgeon General under both Presidents Reagan and George H.W. Bush. Although Houk lived in Atlanta, where the Centers for Disease Control is headquartered, he was fond of holing up in D.C. hotels with multiple bottles of booze and several escorts over the course of a weekend, and Tony was also fully cognizant of the eminent doctor's bacchanal laced sprees.

In the 1980s, Congress tasked Houk with overseeing a study on the toxic effects of Agent Orange on Vietnam veterans, who had been subjected to the carcinogenic chemical en masse. Houk, however, declared that the soldiers' records made it impossible to discern the extent of Vietnam veterans who were subjected to Agent Orange, and he put the kibosh on the study. But a former Chief of Naval Operations, who was the Navy's top commander in

Vietnam, told a House subcommittee that Houk had "made it his mission to manipulate and prevent the true facts from being determined" in his quest to cover up the carnage spawned by Agent Orange. Houk's cover up was also undermined by the Institute of Medicine, an arm of the National Academy of Sciences, which concluded that the Pentagon was fully capable of determining the number of soldiers who had been subjected to Agent Orange, and it also criticized Houk's findings. If Houk had proceeded with the Agent Orange study, the Pentagon undoubtedly would've been liable for astronomical, class-action lawsuits.

Although the government or, perhaps I should say a sinister subgenus of the government, had a vested interest in covering up the evil machinations of Spence et al., the cover up wouldn't have been possible without the collusion of the media, specifically the *Washington Post*. Americans perceive the *Washington Post* as the beacon of truth that ousted the corrupt Nixon administration and saved American democracy. But in my case, the newspaper spearheaded the propaganda campaign of some very powerful, depraved individuals within the government. In previous chapters, I commented on the *Washington Post's* disingenuous deconstruction of the *Washington Times* and also of me. The *Washington Post* was able to impeccably consummate the cover up, because the *New York Times* and the *Los Angeles Times* joined its ranks as it manufactured fabrications that became the recognized reality. I've regrettably learned that truth and the reality manufactured by media are often mutually exclusive.

I've had years to ponder the maliciousness of the media in my case, and I'm nonetheless still at a loss for words. The media has so thoroughly pulverized me that even the slightest vestiges of my humanity have become dust swept away by tempests of deceit. I understand my first barrage of spiteful press in Williamson, because the local funeral homes were protecting their livelihoods, and I understand the *Washington Post's* malice due to the fact that the newspaper was in the midst of protecting an administration and a thoroughly perfidious political machine in which it was a cog.

But the articles concocted about me by West Virginia's media regarding my complicity in Dr. Acosta's tax evasion and also *Funeral Service Insider's* articles seem to be malice for the sake of malice. The grand irony is that the media claims to be an arbitrator of truth and a cornerstone of our democracy, even though the media outlets that have assailed me since the *Washington Post* have merely perpetuated the *Washington Post's* cover up of extremely sordid events that imperil our democracy and also involve the destruction of untold children by dismantling my credibility.

In the midst of a seemingly endless onslaught by the judiciary and the media, I've been awarded a master's degree, and I've transformed myself into a legitimate and very successful businessman. Although I'm a poster boy for a reformed felon, my name nevertheless elicits a feeding frenzy falsehoods.

After my most recent wave of spiteful press and government persecution, my partner said to me that my name is probably irredeemable, and I've also come to the realization that my name very well might be beyond redemption. Nonetheless, I decided to write an accurate account of my life, even though legions of prospective naysayers in the government and media have a vested interest in portraying me as an inveterate criminal and ethical eunuch.

In this book, I have shown numerous examples where the government and media have mass-produced lies about my circumstances and me, especially in Washington, DC. Over the course of writing this book, I've conscripted an attorney to unseal the documents that the government sealed throughout my trial and tribulations in DC. The government gave the attorney a protracted run around for over a year before it declared it was unwilling to unseal various documents related to my case—nearly 25 years after the fact! Until the government is willing to come clean, and unseal all of the documentation in my case, the reader should question the government's veracity before questioning my veracity.

Index